OCCASIONAL PAPER
19

The European Monetary System: The Experience, 1979-82

By Horst Ungerer, with Owen Evans and Peter Nyberg

International Monetary Fund
Washington, D.C.
May 1983

International Standard Serial Number: ISSN 0251-6365

Price: US$5.00
(US$3.00 to university libraries, faculty members,
and students)

Address orders to:
External Relations Department, Attention Publications
International Monetary Fund, Washington, D.C. 20431

Occasional Paper No. 19

The European Monetary System: The Experience, 1979–82

By Horst Ungerer, with Owen Evans and Peter Nyberg
European Department

International Monetary Fund
Washington, D.C.
May 1983

The following symbols have been used throughout this paper:

... to indicate that data are not available;

— to indicate that the figure is zero or less than half the final digit shown, or that the item does not exist;

– between years or months (e.g., 1979–81 or January–June) to indicate the years or months covered, including the beginning and ending years or months;

/ between years (e.g., 1980/81) to indicate a crop or fiscal (financial) year.

"Billion" means a thousand million.

Minor discrepancies between constituent figures and totals are due to rounding.

Contents

		Page
Prefatory Note		v
I.	**Introduction and Background**	1
	History and Objectives	
	Main Features of the EMS	
II.	**The Performance of the System**	4
	General	
	Exchange Rate Developments	
	Variability of Exchange Rates	
	The Problem of Convergence	
	The EMS Concept of Convergence	
	Price Developments	
	Monetary Developments	
	Factors Influencing the Performance of the System	
III.	**The Evolution of the System**	14
	Operational Aspects	
	Exchange Rate and Intervention Mechanism	
	Divergence Indicator	
	Settlement of Intervention Debts	
	Role of the ECU	
	Credit Facilities	
	Proposals for Institutional Changes	
IV.	**The European Monetary System and the International Monetary Fund**	19
	Surveillance over Exchange Rate Policies	
	Conditionality in Credit Operations	
	Creation of International Liquidity	

APPENDICES

I.	**Statistical Tables**	23
II.	**Bibliography**	39

STATISTICAL TABLES

1.	EMS: Periods of Strain	23
2.	EMS: Bilateral Central Rates	24
3.	EMS Realignments: Percentage Changes in Bilateral Central Rates	25

		Page
4.	EMS: ECU Central Rates	25
5.	EMS: Interest Differentials for Three-Month Deposits, 1979–82	26
6.	EMS: Economic Measures in Connection with Realignments	27
7.	Variability of Nominal Effective Exchange Rates, 1974–82	28
8.	Variability of Nominal Exchange Rates Against EMS Currencies, 1974–82	28
9.	Variability of Nominal Exchange Rates Against Non-EMS Currencies, 1974–82	29
10.	Variability of Bilateral Real Exchange Rates Against EMS Currencies, 1974–82	29
11.	Variability of Bilateral Real Exchange Rates Against Non-EMS Currencies, 1974–82	30
12.	Consumer Price Indices, 1974–82	30
13.	GDP Deflators, 1974–81	31
14.	Short-Term Interest Rates, 1974–81	31
15.	Long-Term Interest Rates, 1974–81	32
16.	Matrix of Correlation Coefficients Between Long-Term Interest Rates, March 1976–March 1979 and April 1979–March 1982	32
17.	Matrix of Correlation Coefficients Between Short-Term Interest Rates, March 1976–March 1979 and April 1979–March 1982	33
18.	Rate of Growth of Narrow Money, 1974–81	33
19.	Rate of Growth of Broad Money, 1974–81	34
20.	Rate of Growth of Domestic Credit, 1974–81	34
21.	Real Narrow Money Stock, 1974–81	35
22.	Real Broad Money Stock, 1974–81	35
23.	Real Domestic Credit, 1974–81	35
24.	Central Government Budget Deficit as a Ratio to Nominal GDP, 1974–81	36
25.	Budget Deficits and Changes in Money Supply, 1974–81	36
26.	Balance of Payments Current Account, 1974–81	36
27.	The Creation of ECUs by Swap Operations, April 1979–December 1982	37
28.	Real Rates of Growth of Gross Domestic Product, 1974–81	37
29.	Gross Fixed Capital Formation, 1974–81	38

BIBLIOGRAPHY

CHARTS

Chapter

II.	1. Exchange Rate of the ECU Against the U.S. Dollar	6
	2. Positions Within the EMS Band	7
	3. Movement of EMS Currency Exchange Rates Against the ECU	8
	4. Variability of Nominal Effective Exchange Rates, 1974–82	9
	5. Consumer Prices	11
	6. Changes in Interest Rates and Prices	12
	7. Monetary Expansion Before and After the Introduction of the EMS	13

Prefatory Note

This study was prepared in the European Department of the International Monetary Fund. Its authors are Horst Ungerer, Advisor, and Owen Evans and Peter Nyberg of the Central European Division. The authors are grateful to M. T. Hadjimichael, D. Burton, and T. Juncker for their contributions, and for helpful comments from other staff members.

The present study reviews developments in the European Monetary System from March 1979 to December 1982. As the study was completed in January 1983, it generally does not deal with more recent developments. However, the major realignment of currencies that took place in the European Monetary System on March 21, 1983 has been taken into account where relevant in the text, and the respective tables have accordingly been updated.

Views expressed in the study are those of the authors and do not necessarily represent the views of the Fund.

I. Introduction and Background

This paper is concerned with developments in the European Monetary System (EMS) from its start in March 1979 through December 1982. Chapter I provides a summary of events leading up to the establishment of the EMS and a survey of its main features. Chapter II assesses the performance of the system by describing major exchange rate developments and examining the extent to which exchange rate stability and convergence of economic developments within the EMS have been achieved. Chapter III discusses the evolution of the system with special attention to various operational aspects and a summary of proposals for the institutional development of the system. Chapter IV considers the relationship between the EMS and the International Monetary Fund (IMF). The appendices contain statistical material and a bibliography.

History and Objectives

At its meeting in Bremen on July 6 and 7, 1978, the European Council, composed of the Heads of State and Government of the member countries of the European Community (EC),[1] agreed that closer monetary cooperation between EC countries should be promoted through the creation of the European Monetary System, and an outline for the system was made public as an annex to the conclusions of the Presidency of that meeting. The main features of the EMS were set out in a Resolution adopted by the European Council at its meeting in Brussels on December 4 and 5, 1978.[2] The relevant legal texts, in particular the Agreement between the central banks of the member countries of the EC on the operating procedures for the EMS, were subsequently adopted. The system went into operation as of March 13, 1979, after difficulties relating to monetary aspects of the common agricultural policy of the European Community had been resolved. These difficulties had delayed the entry into force of the EMS from the originally envisaged date of January 1, 1979. At the same time, the European common margins arrangements (the "snake") ceased to exist. All EC member countries but the United Kingdom decided to participate in all aspects of the EMS, in particular in the operational heart of the system, the exchange rate mechanism. Italy and Ireland, due to their particular economic circumstances, at first hesitated to join. However, for economic as well as political reasons, both countries decided in favor of participation. In the case of Italy, the decision to participate was facilitated by the flexibility provided by the possibility offered to EC countries with hitherto floating currencies (i.e., nonparticipants in the "snake") to opt for temporarily wider fluctuation margins (of up to 6 percent instead of 2¼ percent). Ireland joined despite the fact that the United Kingdom decided not to participate in the exchange rate mechanism.

Because the United Kingdom does not participate in the exchange rate mechanism, the link between the British pound and the Irish pound was broken at the end of March 1979. The change encouraged Ireland to orient its economy more toward member countries in the EC other than the United Kingdom. Both Italy and Ireland also benefited from special financial measures for the less prosperous member countries fully participating in the EMS. Greece, which became a member of the European Community as of January 1, 1981, is at present not a member of the EMS.

The United Kingdom accepted general membership in the EMS but decided for the time being not to participate in the exchange rate mechanism; consequently, the Bank of England is not a partner in the very short-term financing facility serving to finance obligatory intervention at the margins in participating currencies. The pound sterling is included in the basket that forms the European Currency Unit (ECU), while the Greek drachma is not; the Treaty of Accession to the EC provides for the inclusion of the drachma, at the latest, by December 31, 1985, or earlier in the case of a revision of the ECU basket.

---

[1] In 1978, the members of the European Community were Belgium, Denmark, France, the Federal Republic of Germany, Ireland, Italy, Luxembourg, the Netherlands, and the United Kingdom. Greece became a member on January 1, 1981.

[2] Relevant documents concerning the EMS have been published by the Commission of the European Communities in: *European Economy*, No. 3 (July 1979). (Hereinafter referred to as *European Economy*, with relevant issue number and date.) For the Resolution see also International Monetary Fund, *IMF Survey*, December 13, 1978, pp. 376–77.

I • INTRODUCTION AND BACKGROUND

The predecessor of the EMS, the European common margins arrangements (the "snake"), was originally part of a broad effort of the EC countries, initiated in 1969, to create an Economic and Monetary Union by 1980. It aimed at the establishment of an autonomous exchange rate system among EC countries and at the gradual abolition of the fluctuation margins between EC currencies. However, adverse events such as the breakdown of the worldwide system of stable exchange rates in 1973 and the first round of oil price increases in 1973–74 (consequences of which differed from country to country) made it difficult for the "snake" to succeed in its original aims. In the end, it was a common exchange rate mechanism for a small group of EC countries (Belgium, Denmark, the Federal Republic of Germany, Luxembourg, and the Netherlands). Over the years, the other EC countries (France, Italy, and the United Kingdom), as well as the two non-EC countries participating in the arrangement, Norway and Sweden, decided to leave the arrangement. While in some aspects, such as the exchange rate mechanism or the financing of intervention, the EMS is broadly similar to the "snake," it differs in other aspects, both technical and political. Above all, the EMS has a political dimension that makes adherence to the system not just a question of economic expediency. Features such as the ECU, the procedures to decide in common about exchange rate changes, and the general emphasis on the convergence of economic policies and developments underline the community aspect of the EMS and the mutual dependence and responsibility of its members.

The main objective of the EMS has been clearly stated by the European Council as a "zone of monetary stability in Europe" (paragraph 1.1 of the Resolution of December 5, 1978) and in the following quotation from the conclusions of the Presidency of the December 1978 meeting:

> The purpose of the European Monetary System is to establish a greater measure of monetary stability in the Community. It should be seen as a fundamental component of a more comprehensive strategy aimed at lasting growth with stability, a progressive return to full employment, the harmonization of living standards and the lessening of regional disparities in the Community. The European Monetary System will facilitate the convergence of economic development and give fresh impetus to the process of European Union. The Council expects the European Monetary System to have a stabilizing effect on international economic and monetary relations....[3]

Main Features of the EMS[4]

At the heart of the EMS is a system of fixed but adjustable exchange rates. Each currency has a central rate expressed in terms of the European Currency Unit (ECU). These central rates determine a grid of bilateral central rates, around which fluctuation margins of ± 2.25 percent (6 percent for the Italian lira) have been established. At these margins, intervention by the participating central banks is obligatory and unlimited in amount. Intervention is, in principle, to be effected in participating currencies;[5] intervention in other currencies (i.e., chiefly in U.S. dollars) is allowed and has been undertaken on a substantial scale.

The grid of bilateral central rates and intervention limits is supplemented by the "divergence indicator," which shows the movement of the exchange rate of each EMS currency against the (weighted) average movement of the other EMS currencies. The criterion used is the divergence of the actual daily rate of the EMS currency, expressed in ECUs, from its ECU central rate. If a currency crosses a "threshold of divergence," set at 75 percent of the maximum divergence spread, this leads to a presumption that the authorities concerned will correct the situation by adequate measures, such as diversified intervention, measures of domestic monetary policy, changes in central rates, or other measures of economic policy.

The ECU plays a central role in the EMS. It serves as the numeraire for the exchange rate mechanism, as the denominator for operations in both the intervention and the credit mechanisms, as a reference point for the divergence indicator, and as a means of settlement and a reserve asset of EMS central banks.

For the financing of interventions in EMS currencies, there are mutual credit lines between the participating central banks (the "very short-term financing facility"). Claims and debts arising from such interventions are settled according to certain rules governing, among other things, the use of ECUs for such purposes.

The "short-term monetary support" and the "medium-term financial assistance," which were established in 1970 and 1971, respectively, were substantially enlarged at the time of establishment of the EMS. They now provide ECU 25 billion[6] of effectively available credit, compared with ECU 10 billion before. The two facilities are available to all members of the EC, including the United Kingdom and Greece. Designed for mutual financial assistance in cases of balance of payments difficulties, they have not been used since the EMS entered into force.

At the start of the EMS, the central banks participating in the exchange rate mechanism of the EMS received an initial supply of ECUs against "contributions" of 20

---

[3] See *European Economy*, No. 3 (July 1979), p. 94.
[4] For details, see International Monetary Fund, *IMF Survey*, March 19, 1979, Supplement: The European Monetary System, pp. 97–100. Additional literature is listed in the bibliography.

[5] Throughout the paper, the terms "participating countries," "participating currencies," "EMS countries," or "EMS currencies" refer to those EC countries or to those currencies of the central banks which are participating in the exchange rate mechanism of the EMS, thus excluding the pound sterling.
[6] ECU 1 = US$0.97 on December 30, 1982.

percent of both their gold holdings and gross U.S. dollar reserves (at market-related valuations) to the European Monetary Cooperation Fund (EMCF).[7] These transactions took the form of revolving three-month swaps, which allow the necessary adjustments to keep contributions at the level of 20 percent each of gold and U.S. dollar reserves, and to take account of any price or rate changes that may have occurred since the previous adjustment. It was agreed that the EMCF would leave the administration of the reserves transferred to it by the swaps to the contributing central banks. The EMCF was established as an institution of the EC in April 1973 and has served as the administrator for transactions under the "snake" and the EMS as well as the very short-term financing facility and the short-term monetary support.

Under the provisions governing the EMS, adjustments of central rates are "subject to mutual agreement by a common procedure which will comprise all countries participating in the exchange rate mechanism and the Commission."[8]

---

[7] The United Kingdom, although not a participant in the exchange rate mechanism, in July 1979 decided to voluntarily contribute 20 percent of its gold and U.S. dollar reserves to the EMCF against ECUs.

[8] European Council Resolution of December 5, 1978, paragraph A.3.2. See *European Economy*, No. 3 (July 1979), p. 95.

II. The Performance of the System

General

At the start of the EMS, contrasting expectations and fears were raised with regard to the consequences of a strict adherence to a system of fixed, though adjustable, exchange rates on economic developments and policies of participating countries. There was concern that the constraints of a system with fixed exchange rates would exert a powerful deflationary influence on economic developments, and that in order to ward off excessive losses of reserves, the countries with higher inflation rates increasingly would be forced to turn to overly restrictive policies, with negative consequences for growth and employment. On the other hand, many critics of the system feared that fixed exchange rates and the consequent obligation to intervene would deprive the more stability-conscious countries of the independence necessary to control domestic monetary expansion so as to contain inflationary price and cost developments. It was argued that the existence of large credit facilities would encourage their use, and that the financing would have to be provided by the countries with stronger currencies, thus allowing the deficit countries to avoid domestic adjustment measures. Such critics feared that the EMS would become a machinery for the creation of more liquidity and inflation and that, even at best, it would force the more stability-conscious countries to settle for a higher average rate of inflation. A third line of thinking was that the system would not be able to hold together for very long. It was unreasonable to expect countries with highly divergent economic developments to be able to align their policies to the degree necessary to keep a system of fixed exchange rates functioning. As a consequence, it was argued, speculative capital movements would disrupt foreign exchange markets and force authorities to make sudden and substantial exchange rate changes with adverse consequences on the economies of participating countries. Hence, the EMS would be faced with problems similar to those that occurred in the final phase of the Bretton Woods system. The only alternative to irregular, sudden, and rather large exchange rate adjustments would be to move to a system with small but frequent exchange rate adjustments—similar to a crawling peg—which would regularly bring exchange rates in line with underlying economic developments. But neither alternative was compatible with one of the basic aims of the EMS, namely, the establishment of a zone of exchange rate stability for the EC as a basis for further economic integration.

Regarding the period under consideration (1979 to 1982), it appears now that many of these concerns were exaggerated. The EMS, in its first years, worked quite smoothly in an operational sense (which in itself is an achievement considering the complex features of the system), and it was, by and large, able to avoid major disruptions. In the years 1979 to 1982, there have been six realignments (Table 3), directly involving from one to four currencies,[9] which were carried out with reasonable smoothness. The first three realignments, in 1979 and early 1981, were certainly not large enough to cause any disruptions in markets; in fact, the changes in central rates were almost fully absorbed by the existing width of the EMS band without significantly affecting market rates. Nor were the adjustments frequent enough to raise doubts about the claim that the system provided a framework for exchange rate stability. The situation has changed somewhat since mid-1981. Tension within the EMS has increased, and, at times, large interventions have been necessary to safeguard existing central rates. Three realignments took place between October 1981 and June 1982. In each, the largest bilateral change of central rates went beyond any previous realignment in the EMS or under the "snake."[10] While in September and November 1979, the maximum bilateral adjustment was 5 percent, it reached more than 9 percent in February and 10½ percent in June 1982. As a result of these three realignments, the central rates of the deutsche mark and the Netherlands guilder rose cumulatively by some 20 percent against the French franc and the Belgian franc. A

---

[9] It should be noted, however, that in an integrated system of a limited number of exchange rates, all participating currencies are affected by action on one or more exchange rates. This is clearly shown by the fact that the adjustment of any number of ECU central rates of EMS currencies leads to simultaneous changes in the ECU central rates of all EMS currencies.

[10] It should be kept in mind, however, that the weaker currencies left the "snake" at various times and subsequently depreciated significantly.

seventh realignment involving all EMS currencies took place on March 21, 1983 in which the largest bilateral adjustment was more than 9 percent.

In general terms, it seems that inflationary impulses have been caused either by events outside the EMS (mainly the second round of oil price increases in 1979–80) or by domestic developments, in particular, budgetary or wage developments; there is little evidence that the EMS caused inflation to be transmitted from one participant to another to a greater extent than would have been the case otherwise.

Equally, it appears that in virtually all EMS countries the impediments to growth stemmed essentially from a recognized need to curb domestic inflation decisively, from a worldwide climate of stagnation, and the requirement to secure overall external balance. In general, these impediments cannot properly be attributed to the consequences of measures introduced to maintain balance within the EMS. To be sure, at times, certain measures, in particular, interest rate actions, were taken in response to temporary developments in the EMS. But it could be said that, in view of the worldwide trend toward higher interest rates and the general need for more restrictive policies in EMS countries, these measures would anyway have had to be introduced, and that at most it was their timing that was influenced by the constraints of the EMS.

Exchange Rate Developments

A number of distinct periods of strain within the EMS can be distinguished (Table 1). During some of these, the authorities attempted to resist changes in central rates by substantial intervention in the exchange market, or by measures of short-term monetary policy directly motivated by exchange rate considerations. Within months of each of these episodes, and in the absence of more far-reaching measures aimed at the correction of the underlying causes of imbalances, confidence in the will and capacity of the authorities to continue to resist the adjustment of central rates diminished, thus amplifying pressure on the exchange rates. In each case, the renewed pressures ended with an adjustment of central rates.

Other periods of strain appear to have followed different patterns. In the case of the devaluation of the Danish krone in November 1979, the authorities acted quickly, without a lengthy period of intervention. On two other occasions, both centered around a weak deutsche mark (October 1980 and February 1981), market pressures were successfully resisted. The ability of the authorities to resist market forces was a reflection of the substantial foreign exchange resources available and, in the second instance, of the forceful measures of monetary policy taken in February 1981. Ultimately, market sentiment reversed itself when it was seen that the Federal Republic of Germany continued to have a better price performance than its partners in the EMS and that an improvement in its current account could be expected.

These experiences appear to be very much in line with those of other countries outside the system: intervention against market pressure serves to buy time, but in the absence of policy measures aimed directly and with sufficient strength at the underlying causes of weakness, exchange rate changes become inevitable in the course of time.

It was early recognized that differences in the relationships between the participating currencies and the U.S. dollar could give rise to tensions within the EMS.[11] When the U.S. dollar is relatively weak, mobile international capital seeks alternative locations, and particularly tends to move to the deutsche mark and vice versa. With the United Kingdom not actively participating in the EMS, currencies other than the deutsche mark play only a limited role as alternative reserve and investment currencies. Consequently, there is a tendency for the deutsche mark to be strong against other European currencies when the U.S. dollar is weak, whether or not underlying economic developments dictate this.

After a short period of strength at the start of the EMS in March 1979, the U.S. dollar remained relatively weak with respect to most EMS currencies from the middle of 1979 to the beginning of 1980 (Chart 1). On September 24, 1979, the first realignment[12] under the EMS occurred with the deutsche mark being revalued by 5 percent against the Danish krone and 2 percent against other EMS currencies. The second realignment occurred on November 30, 1979 when the Danish krone was again devalued by 5 percent against all other currencies.

From early 1980 to early 1981, the U.S. dollar strengthened on average with respect to EMS currencies; there were, however, substantial short-term fluctuations. Early in 1981, an easing of U.S. interest rates and the tightening of monetary policy in the Federal Republic of Germany caused the joint float to firm temporarily relative to the U.S. dollar. An acceleration in inflation and increasing current account difficulties put pressure on the Italian lira within the EMS, triggering substantial intervention by the authorities in February and early March, and leading ultimately to the third realignment, on March 23, 1981, when the lira was devalued by 6 percent relative to the other EMS currencies. The joint float depreciated relative to the U.S. dollar from mid-April until August 1981, with the deutsche mark at the

---

[11] Chart 1 depicts the history of the ECU/dollar rate, and Chart 2 illustrates the positions of the member currencies within the EMS band. Chart 3 shows the ECU exchange rates of the participating currencies.

[12] Detailed information on all the realignments is provided in Tables 3–6. Tables 3–5 provide information on market rates and their changes, and Table 6 outlines policy measures taken in connection with realignments.

II • THE PERFORMANCE OF THE SYSTEM

Chart 1. Exchange Rate of the ECU Against the U.S. Dollar[1]

(In U.S. dollars per ECU)

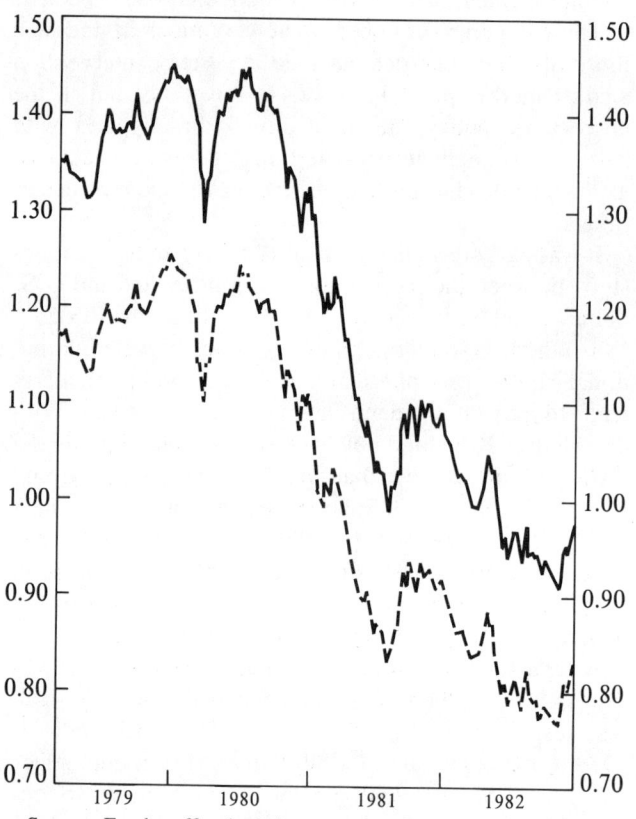

Source: Fund staff calculations.
[1] The lower line excludes the pound sterling component. Calculated from midweek London noon quotations.

top of the band and the French franc at the bottom after its sharp fall following the Presidential elections of May 1981.

From mid-August 1981 to December 1981, the situation reversed with the EMS currencies on average appreciating relative to the U.S. dollar. There was renewed confidence in the deutsche mark as the German current account performance improved and inflation moderated. At the same time, doubts about the stability of the French franc and uncertainties about the policy stance of the new French administration increased. Worsening inflation and a widening trade deficit put renewed pressure on the Italian lira. These tensions led to the fourth realignment, on October 5, 1981, with the deutsche mark and Netherlands guilder revaluing by 5.5 percent, and the French franc and Italian lira devaluing by 3 percent against the Belgian franc, the Luxembourg franc, the Danish krone, and the Irish pound, whose central rates remained unchanged.[13]

[13] The agreement setting up the Belgian-Luxembourg Economic Union (BLEU) entered into force on May 1, 1922 and includes a special protocol providing for a monetary association between the two countries. In accordance with a Luxembourg decree, the Luxembourg franc is at par with the Belgian franc.

The early months of 1982 were characterized by a widening interest rate differential favoring dollar-denominated assets and a firming of the U.S. dollar against the joint float. The Belgian franc came under growing pressure in early February against a background of serious budgetary and current account imbalances and growing external indebtedness. The fifth EMS realignment, effective from February 22, 1982, consisted of an 8.5 percent devaluation of the Belgian franc and Luxembourg franc and a 3.0 percent devaluation of the Danish krone, against all other EMS participants.

Pressure against the French franc, the Belgian franc, and the Italian lira rose again from mid-April 1982. A widening trade deficit and continuing high inflation were major causes. The result was the sixth EMS realignment, effective from June 14, 1982: the French franc and the Italian lira were devalued by 5.75 percent and 2.75 percent, respectively, while the deutsche mark and the Netherlands guilder were revalued by 4.25 percent each against the remaining EMS currencies. This realignment was the largest since the inception of the system in terms of the magnitude of bilateral exchange rate changes.

Since late 1982, continued differences in external and domestic developments and prospects among EMS countries, reflecting divergences in financial policies, were largely responsible for a buildup of exchange rate market tensions and expectations of another realignment. In connection with elections in the Federal Republic of Germany and France in the first half of March 1983, downward pressure on the French franc as well as on the Belgian franc, and upward pressure on the deutsche mark intensified, requiring large-scale intervention. On March 21, 1983, a seventh realignment was agreed upon. The deutsche mark was revalued by 5.5 percent, the Netherlands guilder by 3.5 percent, the Danish krone by 2.5 percent, and the Belgian and Luxembourg francs by 1.5 percent, while the French franc and the Italian lira were devalued by 2.5 percent and the Irish pound by 3.5 percent.

The size and frequency of central rate realignments have increased significantly during the four years of the system's existence. This trend suggests that the drive for greater economic convergence in order to generate exchange rate stability has been successful only to a very limited extent. The increasing size and frequency of realignments also indicate that the disciplinary effect of fixed exchange rates is not itself sufficient but that, additionally, determined and sustained domestic adjustment efforts are required.

A variety of policy measures has accompanied EMS realignments (Table 6), but only at the realignment in June 1982 were the accompanying measures directly stated in the communiqué announcing the realignment. On that occasion, there was explicit mention of the measures that France would take, as well as of the less precisely specified measures that Italy would adopt. This

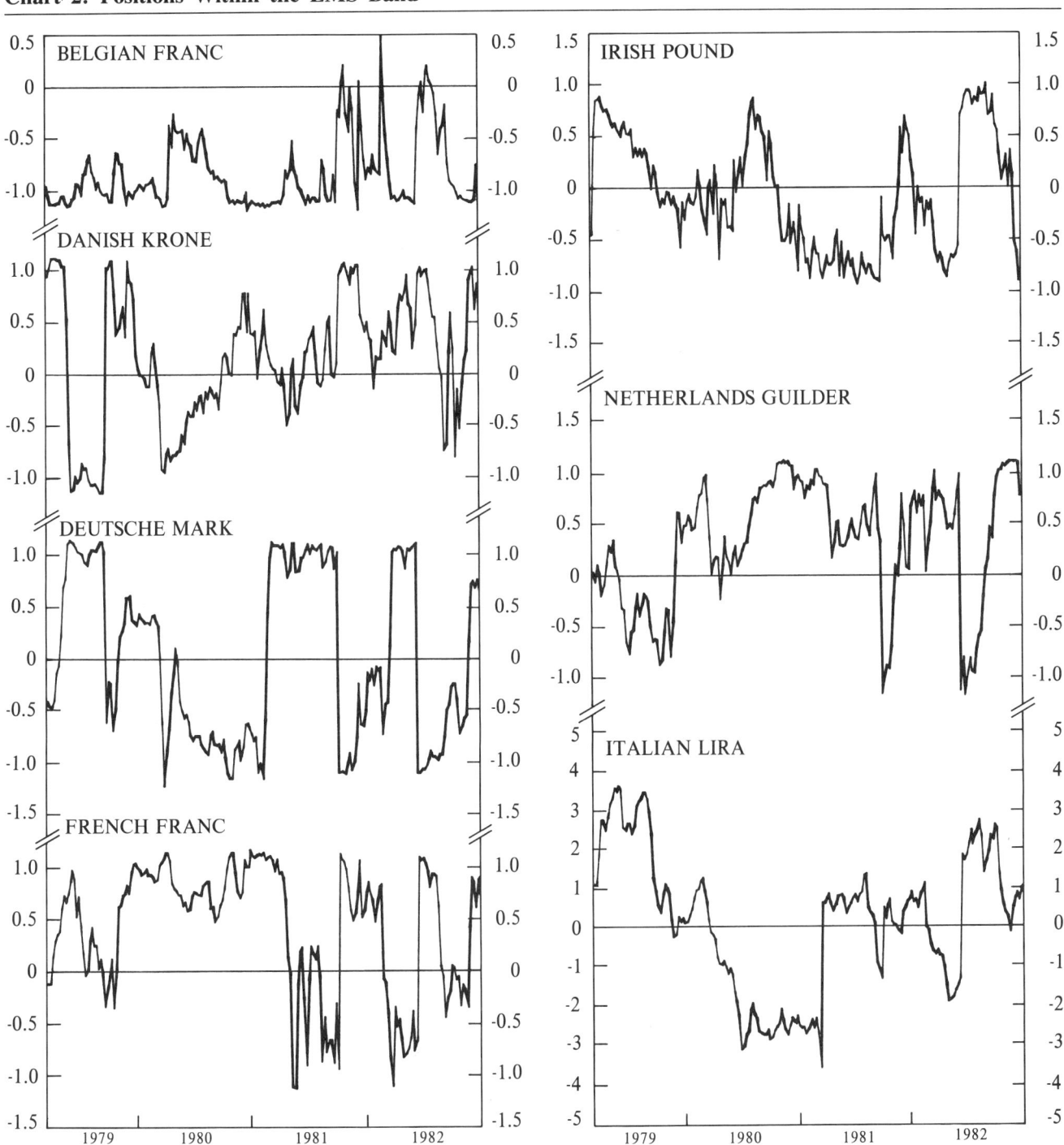

Chart 2. Positions Within the EMS Band[1]

Source: Fund staff calculations.
[1] Deviations from central positions (average of the highest and lowest spreads) within the narrow EMS band.

does not, of course, mean that other realignments have remained unsupported by economic measures. The devaluation of the Danish krone in November 1979 was part of a larger package of policy measures, as was the case with the devaluation of the Belgian franc in February 1982, and those of the French franc in October 1981 and of the Italian lira in March and October 1981. In March 1983, following the realignment, France adopted a package of restrictive budgetary and monetary measures as well as restrictions on expenditure for foreign travel.

II • THE PERFORMANCE OF THE SYSTEM

Chart 3. Movement of EMS Currency Exchange Rates Against the ECU[1]
(Monthly averages, March 1979 = 100)

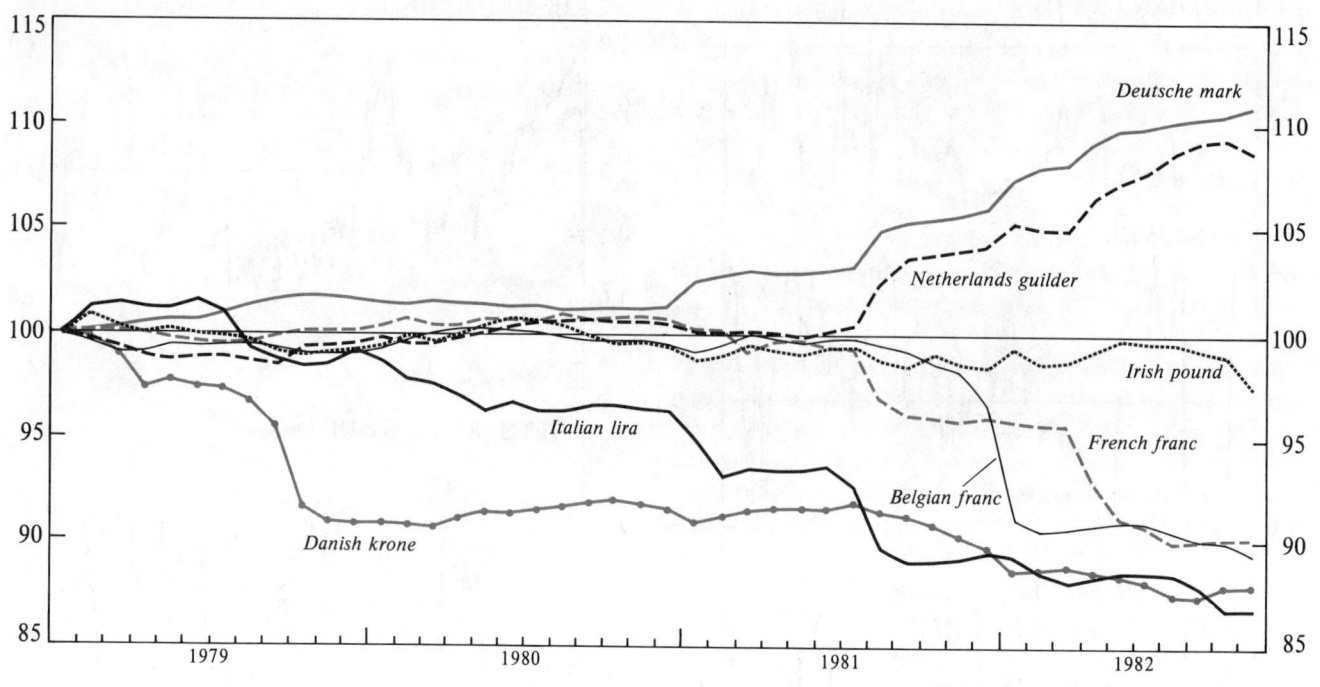

Sources: Commission of the European Communities and Fund staff calculations.
[1] ECU without pound sterling component.

Variability of Exchange Rates

Foremost among the objectives of the EMS is the achievement of a high degree of exchange rate stability as a basis for further economic integration. It is chiefly this objective that is supported by the institutional arrangements of the EMS. Central rate changes are subject to a multilevel consultation and decision-making process; furthermore, the implications of such changes on other aspects of EC policies need to be taken into account. At the beginning of the EMS, all this had led to the fear that needed exchange rate changes might not be undertaken in time nor to the extent required. The danger of competitive devaluations, on the other hand, was seen as remote.

In the event, the exchange rate system of the EMS proved to be much less rigid than initially feared. More recently, following the relatively large realignments since October 1981, voices have been raised querying whether exchange rate changes have not been used too much, instead of stronger domestic adjustment measures and greater efforts to achieve more convergence in economic policies and developments. It is being asked whether too frequent changes in official exchange rates did not erode a system that was intended to create "a zone of monetary stability" in Europe.

The question of the degree of exchange rate stability achieved in the EMS may be approached first by comparing the experience of the EMS countries among themselves before and after the implementation of the system. Secondly, exchange rate stability for the currencies in the EMS can be compared with those of major currencies outside the EMS. This section examines the variability of both real and nominal exchange rates before and after the establishment of the EMS in March 1979. The question at issue is whether or not the EMS has had a stabilizing effect on the exchange rates of the participating currencies. Ideally, variability should be measured relative to the equilibrium exchange rate over time for a currency, but this is well beyond the scope of this paper. Here, variability is measured by the coefficient of variation (standard deviation divided by the average) over a sample period. The variability of exchange rates of EMS currencies can then be compared both before and after the introduction of the system and with the variability of the exchange rates of non-EMS currencies over the same periods. Clearly, such comparisons are sensitive to the choice of comparator currencies, to the frequency of the data, and to the exchange rate measure used. Because of this, results are reported for differing time intervals and for several different measures of exchange rates. Nevertheless, the results should be interpreted cautiously. A particularly important qualification is that the exchange rate experience of European currencies before the introduction of the EMS varied markedly, with the role played by the "snake" being of notable importance.

The variability of exchange rates of EMS currencies in the period 1979 to 1982 appears to have declined, compared with a number of non-EMS currencies inside and outside Europe (Chart 4). For all EMS currencies, except the Danish krone, average variability in 1979–81 was less than that in 1974–78 (Table 7).[14] It may at first appear surprising that the average variability of the nominal effective exchange rates of the five non-EMS European countries considered (Austria, Norway, Sweden, Switzerland, and the United Kingdom) declined by a similar degree as the EMS currencies over 1979–81, compared to 1974–78. On reflection, this is less so, given the close economic and financial ties between many European countries, whether EMS participants or not, and given the formalization of these links in the exchange rate regimes of several of the countries concerned. The exchange rate of the Austrian schilling is closely associated with the EMS currencies, in particular, the deutsche mark, and the exchange rate for the Swiss franc, although largely market determined, is heavily influenced by developments in the EMS. Both Norway and Sweden peg their exchange rates to baskets of currencies in which the combined weight of EMS currencies is 44 percent (for Norway it was 33 percent before August 1982).[15]

Of the non-EMS European currencies considered, only the pound sterling is less dependent, directly or indirectly, on the behavior of EMS participants. Consequently, it is to be expected that the pound sterling is the only European currency under consideration, inside or outside the EMS, to exhibit a major rise in average exchange rate variability after the system's introduction (Table 7).

Predictably, the average variability of each of the EMS member currencies with respect to the rest of the EMS group diminished after the introduction of the system (Table 8). This is presumably the minimum achievement one would expect. The variability of the non-EMS European currencies considered (with the exception of the pound sterling) relative to the EMS group also diminished after the system's inception (although to a lesser degree) which could be expected since these currencies are closely linked to the EMS currencies. On the other hand, the average variability of the exchange rates for the U.S. dollar and the Japanese yen relative to the EMS group increased sharply after the introduction of the system. The variability of the non-EMS currencies considered relative to their own group has also risen somewhat since the inception of the EMS (Table 9).

The real exchange rates[16] of EMS countries have, as well, become less variable relative to their own group (Table 10) and more variable relative to currencies outside the joint float (Table 11), since the system was instituted.

In sum, it appears that the exchange rate variability of the EMS currencies has diminished since the introduction of the system, and that this stabilizing influence has spread to the exchange rates of the currencies of those European countries outside the EMS which have close economic and financial ties to EMS participants. In contrast, the exchange rate variability of the major currencies not tied to the EMS (the pound sterling, the U.S. dollar, and the Japanese yen) appears to have risen significantly.

Chart 4. Variability of Nominal Effective Exchange Rates, 1974–82[1]

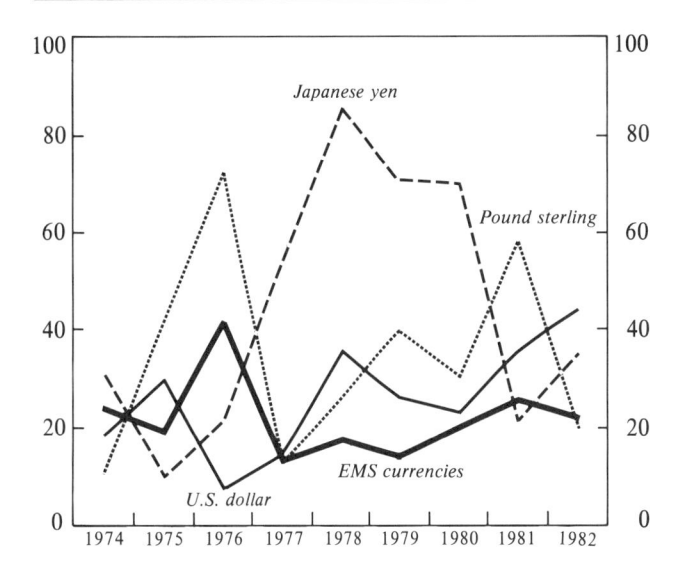

Sources: International Monetary Fund, *International Financial Statistics;* and Fund staff calculations.
[1] Variability is measured by the coefficient of variation (standard deviation divided by the average) multiplied by 1000, of the nominal effective exchange rate. The variability of EMS currencies is measured by the simple average of variability of nominal effective exchange rates of participants.

---

[14] In Chart 4 and Table 7, variability is measured by 1,000 times the coefficient of variation of the nominal effective exchange rate (monthly data).

[15] If the indirect effects of EMS exchange rates on third currencies also in the baskets were taken into account, these shares would be even higher.

[16] In a way, the behavior of real exchange rates is not relevant here since the stabilizing effect of a system with fixed exchange rates affects in the short run only nominal exchange rates. On the other hand, developments of real exchange rates reveal whether divergencies between exchange rates and cost and price developments arise or whether such divergencies have been compensated for by changes in central rates. Hence, developments in real exchange rates can be seen as composite indicators for the stability of nominal exchange rates and the achievement of convergence in cost and price developments.

II • THE PERFORMANCE OF THE SYSTEM

The Problem of Convergence

The EMS Concept of Convergence

The concept of convergence, which has become widely used in the context of economic integration, needs to be given some precision of meaning. In general, convergence means a development in which economic variables move closer to each other over time. By itself, however, the concept of convergence neither identifies the variables under consideration nor the direction of their movements.[17]

The ultimate aim of the European Community in the economic field is, according to the Preamble to the European Economic Community Treaty, "to ensure the economic and social progress of their countries..." and "the constant improvement of the living and working conditions of their peoples."[18] From the beginning of the EC, there have been efforts to reduce regional disparities among member countries. The lending activities of the European Investment Bank (EIB), the European Social Fund, the European Regional Development Fund, and—more recently—the New Community Instrument ("Ortoli facility") are directed toward these aims. In connection with the establishment of the EMS, it was decided to lend support to strengthening the economic potential of those less prosperous member countries which fully participate in the EMS by subsidizing interest rates on loans from the EIB and the New Community Instrument.[19] Italy and Ireland are the countries benefiting from those measures.

A reduction of disparities among EC member countries is, however, a goal in itself and not necessarily a condition for economic integration. Disparities are present within individual countries and sometimes are as pronounced as among different countries. By contrast, it has long been recognized that economic and/or monetary integration requires a certain degree of "harmonization" or "convergence" in economic policies and developments. While the EMS is expected to contribute to the longer-term aims of the EC, it has as its specific aim the creation of "a zone of monetary stability in Europe," encompassing "greater stability at home and abroad."[20] "Stability abroad" is equivalent to exchange rate stability, and from many references, it is clear that "[monetary] stability at home" is to be interpreted as domestic monetary developments consistent with stability of costs and prices.[21] Both the stability of exchange rates as well as that of costs and prices are seen as essential preconditions for further economic integration among EC countries for future economic growth and the narrowing of differences in living standards.

It had been hoped that the EMS would promote greater convergence of economic policies and developments and eventually facilitate economic integration. So far, however, such hopes have not been fulfilled as convergence of policies, particularly budgetary and monetary policies, has been insufficient to maintain a high degree of exchange rate stability. The lack of coordination of policies has been reflected in a lack of convergence of economic performance and, in particular, of cost and price developments. An opinion held by many, however, is that the existence of and the constraints imposed by the EMS have helped to prevent a greater divergence of economic developments in the participating countries.

While the following summarily reviews price and monetary developments, reference is made to more detailed studies by the EC Commission and various authors.[22]

Price Developments

The level and dispersion of inflation rates is of central importance for evaluating the extent of convergence toward monetary stability within the EMS. In 1979, the preconditions for convergence appeared to be improving both within and outside the EC. Inflation rates had been dropping or stabilizing since 1975, both in terms of consumer prices and gross domestic product (GDP) deflators. At the same time, differences between the highest and the lowest inflation rate of the member countries were diminishing and reached their minimum in 1978 (Table 12).

The launching of the EMS roughly coincided with the second major oil price increases, which caused an intensification of inflationary pressures. The response to these pressures varied considerably between countries,

---

[17] The Commission of the European Communities introduced a useful distinction between "convergence of nominal variables," such as costs and prices, and "convergence of real variables," such as living standards and quality of life. See *European Economy*, No. 12 (July 1982), p. 14. This publication contains many documents and technical studies relating to the EMS.

[18] European Communities, *Treaties Establishing the European Communities: Treaties Amending These Treaties; Documents Concerning the Accession* (Luxembourg, 1973), p. 173.

[19] See December 5, 1978 Resolution of the European Council, Section B in *European Economy*, No. 3 (July 1979), p. 97.

[20] See December 5, 1978 Resolution in *European Economy*, No. 3 (July 1979), p. 95.

[21] See, for example, "Conclusions of the Presidency" of the European Council Meeting in Luxembourg, April 27–28, 1980, in: *Bulletin of the European Communities*, No. 4 (1980), p. 10; *European Economy*, No. 12 (July 1982), pp. 14, 40, and 42; and *European Economy*, No. 14 (November 1982), p. 94.

[22] See, for example, *European Economy* (July 1982), "Part One - Economic Convergence and the European Monetary System," Michael Emerson, "European Dimensions in the Problems of Adjustment," *European Monetary System and International Monetary Reform*, Editions de l'Université de Bruxelles (Brussels, 1981), pp. 107–38, and Niels Thygesen, "Are Monetary Policies and Performances Converging?" (with a comment by Wolfgang Rieke) in "The European Monetary System: The First Two Years," Banca Nazionale del Lavoro, *Quarterly Review* (September 1981), pp. 297–326.

leading to a renewed increase in inflation differentials. Thus, while consumer prices in the Federal Republic of Germany rose by 16.3 percent from 1978 to 1981, they increased by 37.5 percent in Denmark, 42.2 percent in France, and 63.9 percent in Italy. By the end of 1982, a major convergence of inflation rates was not yet in sight. However, inflation differentials had fallen somewhat from their 1980 levels.

Inflationary developments in selected countries outside the EMS since 1979 were broadly similar. The differences in inflation rates were, however, not as pronounced as those within the EMS (Chart 5 and Tables 12–13).

Monetary Developments

Since 1979, very pronounced and similar rises in nominal domestic interest rates have taken place in the countries concerned, partly in response to the large interest rate increases in the United States. In most countries participating in the EMS, nominal interest rates were 2–4 percentage points higher in 1979–81 than in 1976–78. Because interest rate changes in the medium term were unrelated to actual changes in inflation rates (Chart 6 and Tables 12–15), real interest rates generally increased most in countries with decreasing or stable rates of inflation. The rise in real interest rates was especially sharp in Belgium, Denmark, the Federal Republic of Germany, and the Netherlands, while the increases were less pronounced in France, Ireland, and Italy.

During 1979–82, there was a definite increase in the correlation between interest rate movements in countries participating in the European Monetary System (Tables 16–17). While interest rate developments in the United States played a significant role, a substantial part of the convergence of interest rates within the EMS can be attributed to monetary measures following the establishment of the EMS. Larger EMS countries, especially the Federal Republic of Germany, have used the rate of growth of monetary aggregates as normative, intermediate goals of monetary policy. As stability of the exchange rate is especially important for the smaller EMS countries with very open economies, monetary policy in these countries has often been geared to maintain this stability. While this has resulted in a tendency to equalize interest rate developments within the EMS, monetary expansion within the small countries has remained partly outside the control of the national authorities.

The medium-term rise in interest rates in most EMS countries has been accompanied by a decelerating growth of the nominal money supply (Chart 7 and Tables 18–19). The change in the growth rate of both narrow and broad money was, however, very different in individual countries.

Chart 5. Consumer Prices
(Second quarter 1979 = 100)

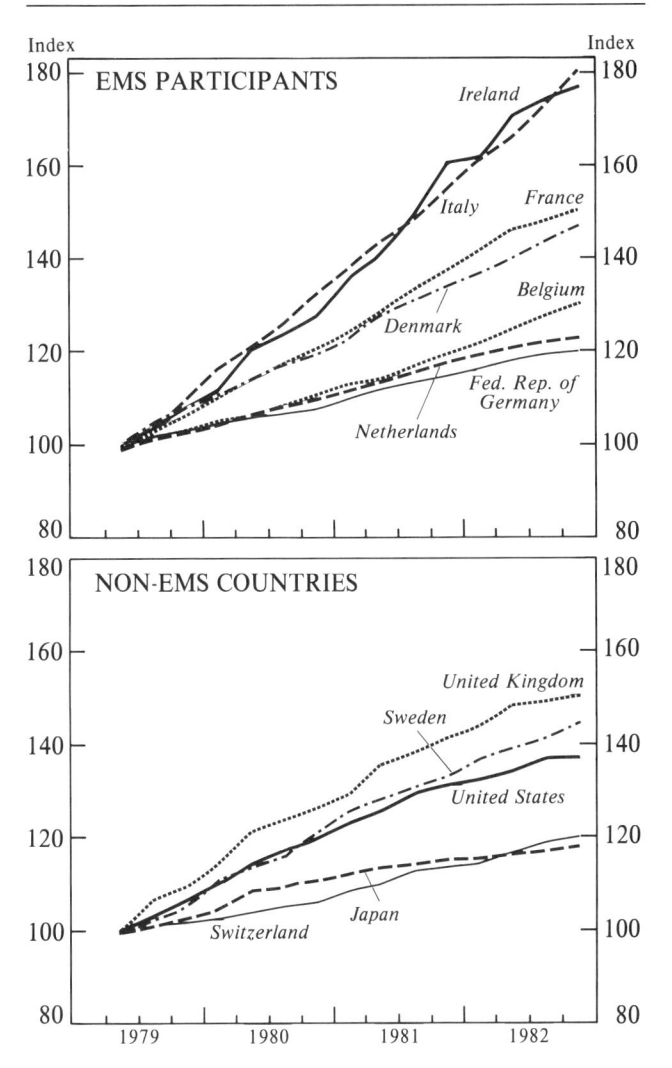

Source: International Monetary Fund, *International Financial Statistics*.

The rate of domestic credit expansion is perhaps of greater interest as an indicator of the determination and success of the authorities in controlling monetary developments (Chart 7 and Table 20). This rate is, like those for other monetary aggregates, quite different in the various participating countries. Developments appear, however, to have converged somewhat during the first years of the European Monetary System. In all participating countries (with the exception of Denmark) credit expansion was then, on average, slower than or about the same as that experienced in the period 1974–78. The rate of domestic credit expansion has generally decreased more for countries with a high rate of expansion in the period preceding the introduction of the EMS.

The development of the real money or credit supply is often considered a more reliable indicator of monetary

II • THE PERFORMANCE OF THE SYSTEM

Chart 6. Changes in Interest Rates and Prices[1]
(Average change from 1974–78 to 1979–81 in percentage points)

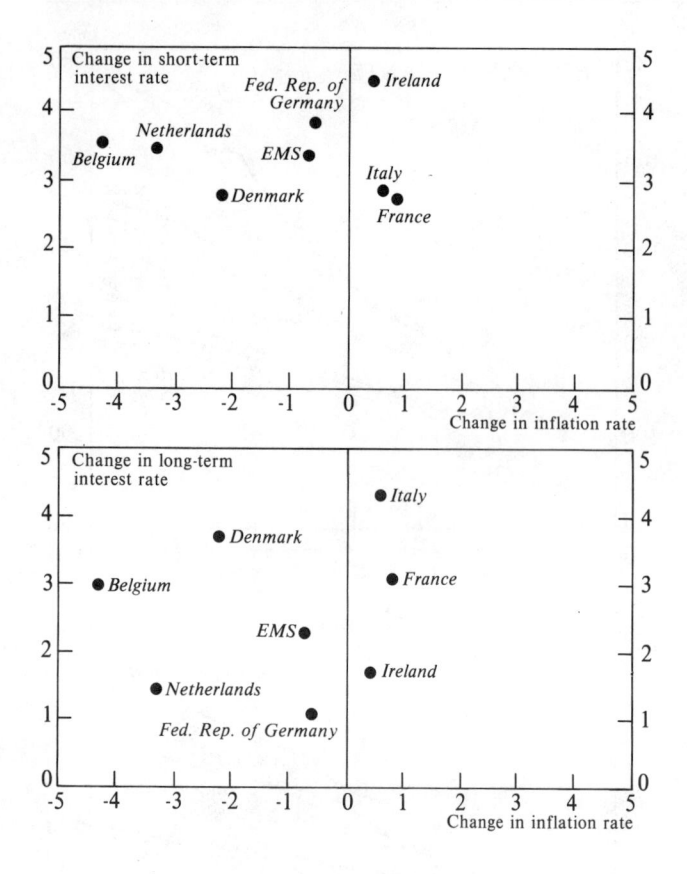

Sources: International Monetary Fund, *International Financial Statistics*, and Fund staff calculations.

[1] Vertical axis: change in average interest rates from 1974–78 to 1979–81. Horizontal axis: change in GDP deflator from 1974–78 to 1979–81. The higher up and more to the left a country lies in the diagram, the more real interest rates have increased.

stringency than the expansion of purely nominal variables. Deflating the monetary aggregates with the GDP deflator produces measures of real monetary expansion which are as widely divergent during 1979–81 as before. On the other hand, correcting monetary developments for changes in the consumer price index (Tables 21–23) indicates that the rates of real monetary expansion have been, on average, more similar in 1979–81 than in 1974–78 (the evidence being weakest in the case of credit expansion).[23]

During the first years of the EMS, there was also a general rise in the general government borrowing requirements of EMS countries relative to increases in the money supply (Table 25). These developments to a large extent reflect the result of the "automatic" effects of the onset of recession in 1980 on tax receipts and transfer outlays, as well as the different timing and impact of financial policies as the recession developed.

Factors Influencing the Performance of the System

As shown above, the trend toward a higher degree of convergence in economic performance among EMS countries, which was evident mainly in price performance during the two years prior to the establishment of the EMS, did not continue afterwards but rather reversed itself. In particular, inflation differentials between the Federal Republic of Germany and the Netherlands, on the one hand, and France and Italy, on the other hand, grew larger over time. These divergences would have been expected to create major tension within the EMS. Expectations at the outset were that the deutsche mark would remain strong within the EMS, while concern over future developments concentrated on the French franc and the Italian lira. However, the EMS operated smoothly and free of major disruptions, at least up to mid-1981.

After May 1980, the deutsche mark weakened within the EMS, and somewhat later, in line with the EMS as a whole, it weakened also against the dollar. One important factor in this development was the current account development in the Federal Republic of Germany. It deteriorated dramatically from the second quarter of 1979 not only because of the changing relative cyclical position and a delayed response to the deterioration of competitiveness, but also, as in the case of other EMS countries, because of the second round of sharp oil price increases. The impact of current account developments on exchange rates was exacerbated by developments in the capital account. The reputation of the deutsche mark as a steadily appreciating currency, and thus as a safe alternate reserve and investment currency, was undermined. Interest rate developments contributed to pressure on the deutsche mark while supporting the U.S. dollar as well as other EMS currencies, such as the French franc. Lastly, there were political developments that cast a spell over the deutsche mark and favored the U.S. dollar as well as, temporarily, the French franc.

The authorities of various EMS countries have also on several occasions taken external or domestic measures designed to cope with the consequences of divergence, to ensure some degree of convergence or at least avoid more divergent developments. The existence of the EMS and the resulting exchange rate constraint in some countries have induced (and have been used in the public debate as an argument for) a stronger domestic adjustment effort by modifying wage indexation provisions (Belgium, Denmark, and Italy) or by introducing more restrictive budget policies (Belgium, Denmark, and France).

---

[23] Because annual expansion rates have continued to fluctuate widely for individual countries, average annual dispersion measures, nevertheless, remain high.

Chart 7. Monetary Expansion Before and After the Introduction of the EMS[1]

(Average annual change for 1974–78 and 1979–81 in percent)

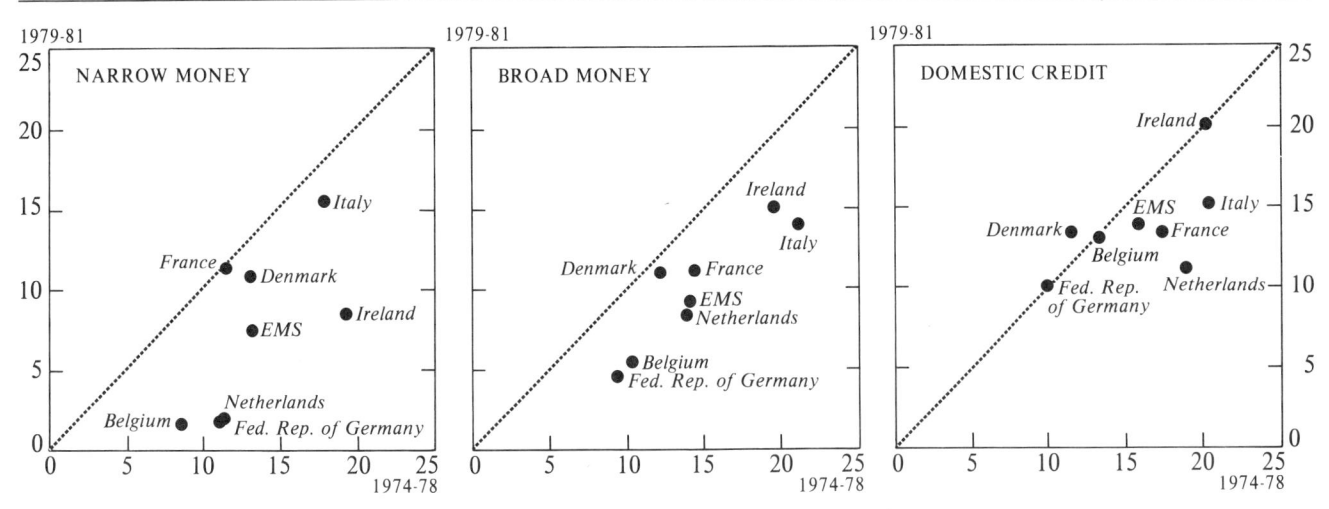

Sources: International Monetary Fund, *International Financial Statistics,* and Fund staff calculations.

[1] Countries on the diagonal have the same average monetary expansion rates in 1979–81 as in 1974–78. Countries below (above) the diagonal have a lower (higher) rate of monetary expansion in 1979–81 than in 1974–78. The greater the distance from the diagonal the greater is the difference in the average rate of monetary expansion between the two periods.

The initial moderating effects that contributed to a smooth beginning of the EMS have dissipated, however; no clear signs of a noticeable convergence of economic policies and developments could be detected; and recourse to measures to temporarily mitigate balance of payments difficulties (such as interest rate changes or foreign borrowing) may become more difficult. As a result, it might well be that tensions within the EMS increase. It appears that, in principle, the following main options for action remain open to the authorities of EMS countries, short of abandoning the EMS in its present form. On the one hand, further changes in EMS exchange rates may have to be made. On the other hand, more substantial domestic adjustment programs will have to be put in place by the countries with less stable currencies and with serious payments problems as it seems difficult to imagine that the more stability-oriented countries will be prepared to compromise their policy stance and agree to an "average" degree of convergence in terms of monetary expansion and inflation. The countries under pressure could combine medium-term programs for stabilizing and restructuring their economies with recourse to longer-term external financing. It is also obvious that the first option, more frequent exchange rate action, would nevertheless require supportive domestic measures to ensure success.

III. The Evolution of the System

Operational Aspects

The European Council Resolution of December 5, 1978 established the framework for the European Monetary System and the Agreement of March 13, 1979 between the EC central banks provided the operating procedures. The operation of the EMS from the beginning has been characterized by two elements: it has been flexible in many of its technical aspects, and it has been run efficiently and smoothly by the participating central banks. The Central Bank Agreement was never intended to lay down rigid and unalterable rules for the system. The wording of the Agreement leaves room for flexibility and thus allows a gradual evolution of the system over time as experience is gained. In some important aspects of the system (such as currency of intervention, maturity of credits, or means for settlement of such credits), the provisions of the Agreement apply only "in principle," leaving open the choice of mutually agreed ways to be used in handling new problems.

This high degree of flexibility can be explained by a number of factors. The EMS—as is true for many aspects of EC policies—is primarily an institution not so much of a technical but mainly of a political nature, where technical means are used toward political objectives. It may be seen as an important step on the way to a much more ambitious but also fairly distant goal: monetary union. The flexibility of the system was seen as necessary because of varying institutional settings and different approaches to many common problems among the participating central banks; it is workable because the central banks concerned, which are limited in number, have a long-standing tradition of close cooperation in foreign exchange matters, stemming, in particular, from the operation of the "snake." The Committee of Governors of the central banks of the EC and its working parties meet regularly and frequently, normally in Basle, in connection with the monthly meetings of the Bank for International Settlements (BIS). All questions that arise in connection with the functioning of the system, be they of a more technical nature or touching upon more fundamental questions of external or domestic monetary policy, are discussed during these meetings. The four daily telephone consultations between all EC central banks on exchange rate matters usually provide, on the level of foreign exchange departments, an exchange of information on market developments and intervention activities and offer a readily available channel for consultation on higher levels as the need arises. (The central banks of Norway, Sweden, Switzerland, and the Federal Reserve Bank of New York, as well as, less directly, the central banks of Canada and Japan, are associated with this network of information.) The Monetary Committee of the EC regularly brings together high officials from central banks and finance ministries. The central bank governors also frequently attend meetings of economics and finance ministers of the EC member countries. The EC Commission is represented on the appropriate level on all the committees and at all the meetings which have been mentioned.

The following sections describe the evolution of some key operational features of the EMS. The survey is neither exhaustive, nor, in all respects, completely up-to-date because many aspects remain in flux and some details may not be known, due to their confidential nature.

Exchange Rate and Intervention Mechanism

The Central Bank Agreement stipulates that intervention be effected, in principle, in currencies of the participating central banks and be unlimited in amount at the obligatory intervention limits. This provision allows intervention in third currencies which normally takes place before the intervention limits are reached. It also allows intervention in participating currencies before the intervention limit is reached ("intramarginal intervention"), which is, however, subject to prior approval of the partner central bank in whose currency intervention is to take place.

In the first three years of the EMS, more than half of intervention by EMS participants has been effected in third currencies, predominantly in U.S. dollars. This is due to a number of reasons. At first, such intervention may have primarily, but neither necessarily nor exclusively, served the purpose of influencing the exchange rate relationship between the currency of the intervening central bank and the third currency in question. Secondly, a number of central banks prefer to intervene before their currency reaches its obligatory intervention limits because they want to avoid larger fluctuations, even within the band of the EMS. Or, the central banks may intervene because they consider it important to counter exchange rate movements at the beginning before they gather momentum; in this way, they may hope to achieve their exchange rate objectives with a smaller change in their reserve position. For such purposes, these central banks may use U.S. dollars for intervention instead of intramarginal intervention in participating currencies, since the latter requires the consent of the central bank whose currency is being used. The Italian authorities, in view of the wider fluctuation margins of 6 percent for the Italian lira, have consistently followed a policy of not allowing their currency to reach its intervention limits, and have consequently intervened in U.S. dollars (see Chart 2).

Of intervention in EMS currencies during the first three years, again more than half consisted of intramarginal intervention. Since the automatic financing provisions of the very short-term facility apply only to obligatory intervention at the limits, a central bank that would like to intervene intramarginally in another EMS currency would at first need to have a sufficient amount of the currency in question at its disposal. While this could be done by acquiring such currency on the market during earlier periods of strength, the Central Bank Agreement limits the holding of such currencies to working balances. Alternatively, the central bank would have to obtain the currency by agreement from the issuing central bank. Such agreements have at times been concluded when the interests of the two central banks could be reconciled, for instance, in the form of swap agreements that allowed a reversal of the transaction after a certain time. For the creditor central bank, such an agreement had the desirable effect of also canceling the liquidity-creating effect of the initial intervention. The choice of intervention currency is, of course, of interest with regard to its consequences on the overall creation of international liquidity and its impact on the exchange rates of the currencies involved.

Divergence Indicator

In the early phases of discussions about the EMS, there was a proposal that the exchange rate mechanism should be based not on a grid of bilateral parities—as it was in the "snake"—but directly on the ECU. Under such a system, for each currency a central rate in terms of the ECU would be declared, and fluctuation margins would be defined against the ECU, instead of against other currencies; countries would be obliged to keep their currencies within these margins. In the event, this idea was not accepted, mainly for two reasons. The first one is of a general nature. While such a system, requiring any central bank to intervene whose currency diverges by a given margin from its ECU central rate, would support efforts to achieve a higher degree of convergence, it would do so irrespective of the desired direction of convergence. Secondly, as a technical point, though with important policy implications, there would be the problem of determining the "partner" currency for intervention. Since, under such a system, frequently only one currency would reach its intervention point in terms of the ECU, the selected or designated intervention partner would become an "involuntary" creditor who would have to accept the creation of more liquidity in its own currency, or an "involuntary" debtor who would have to suffer the loss of reserves. In the end, the parity grid became the basis for the exchange rate and intervention mechanism, and the ECU-based divergence indicator became a supplementary device, functioning as a warning system. By inviting consultations and creating a "presumption" for corrective action, the indicator became a factor in promoting policy coordination.

Nevertheless, the role of the divergence indicator remains ambiguous. While being in line with the desire expressed in the Resolution of December 5, 1978, to balance the burden of both deficit and surplus countries, the indicator has a built-in tendency to promote convergence not necessarily toward monetary stability but rather toward some average level of monetary and price developments. This ambiguity may have been one reason why the divergence indicator appears not to have played the role it was expected to play. There are other reasons, some of them of a more technical nature. First, signals of the divergence indicator cannot automatically trigger action, but can only attempt to induce such action. Second, the very design of the indicator, based on a composite of all the currencies, causes it to respond only in situations where one currency is clearly divergent from the average of the other currencies. If two currencies would strongly move in opposite directions, it is most likely that neither currency would cross its divergence threshold. This explains also why, in certain cases, a currency may reach its intervention limit under the parity grid before reaching the divergence threshold, thus diminishing the ability of the divergence indicator to act as an "early warning system." Lastly, the inclusion of the pound sterling, which does not participate in the exchange rate mechanism of the EMS, in the ECU as well as the application of wider margins for the Italian lira, have at times resulted in some distortions, in spite of the adjustments in the calculation of the divergence indicator eliminating the movements of these currencies beyond their notional 2.25 percent margins.[24]

---

[24] For details see International Monetary Fund, *IMF Survey* (March 19, 1979), *Supplement: The European Monetary System*, p. 98. For further literature on the functioning of the divergence indicator, see bibliography, in particular, Jean-Jacques Rey, "Some Comments on the Merits and Limits of the Indicator of Divergence of the European Monetary System," *Revue de la Banque*, No. 1 (1982), pp. 3-15 and Joanne Salop, "The Divergence Indicator: A Technical Note," International Monetary Fund, *Staff Papers*, Vol. 28 (December 1981), pp. 682-97.

III • THE EVOLUTION OF THE SYSTEM

During a review of the EMS conducted in September 1979, it was decided not to modify the functioning of the divergence indicator. It would have been possible to increase the likelihood of the indicator signaling a currency as being divergent before it would reach its bilateral intervention limits by lowering the divergence threshold significantly, for example, from 75 to 50 percent. However, this would have meant that the indicator's warning bell would ring quite frequently—often without justification—causing the authorities to pay less attention to it.

Settlement of Intervention Debts

According to the Central Bank Agreement, the time for the settlement of claims and debts from obligatory intervention in participating currencies of debts under the very short-term financing facility is 45 days after the end of the month in which intervention took place. This can be extended automatically by three months, subject to certain limitations, and by another three months, subject to the agreement of the creditor central bank. Settlement is to be effected:

— in the first place by using holdings in the creditor currencies;
— subsequently in part or wholly in ECUs, with the proviso that a creditor central bank is not obliged to accept settlement in ECUs of an amount exceeding 50 percent of its claim;
— for the remaining balance in other reserve assets in accordance with the composition of the debtor central bank's reserves, excluding gold.

The Agreement, however, explicitly leaves room for other forms of settlement as agreed between creditor and debtor central banks.

In practice, various methods have been used to settle claims and debts arising from intervention. The very short-term financing facility, which applies only to obligatory intervention, has not been used extensively, and the formal settlement procedures as outlined above have been applied only to a relatively small part of intervention debts. The larger part of debts and claims resulting from obligatory intervention have been offset against each other, or settled by the debtor central bank buying the currency of the creditor. The latter method has the advantage of influencing the money supply of the creditor country only temporarily and was frequently facilitated by extending the settlement date automatically or by mutual agreement.

A substantial part of intervention in currencies of participating central banks was intramarginal and largely financed by using holdings of the intervention currency which had been acquired earlier in the markets or resulted from borrowing abroad. Another part was financed by spot settlement in U.S. dollars or ECUs.

Role of the ECU

At the start of the EMS, each central bank participating in the exchange rate mechanism was to contribute 20 percent of its gold holdings and 20 percent of its gross reserves in U.S. dollars to the European Monetary Cooperation Fund (EMCF). Against these contributions, the EMCF issued a corresponding amount of ECUs. These transactions took the form of revolving three-month swaps. For the purpose of these transactions, U.S. dollars are valued at the market rate, and gold at the average market price of the six previous months or of the two fixings on the penultimate working day, whichever is lower. Every three months, the necessary adjustments are made to ensure that contributions continue to represent at least 20 percent of the gold and U.S. dollar reserves of the participating central banks and to bring the amount of issued ECUs in line with changed valuations.

At the beginning of the EMS, ECU 23 billion were created. When, in July 1979, the United Kingdom decided to voluntarily contribute 20 percent of its gold and U.S. dollar reserves, the amount increased to ECU 27 billion. Subsequently, the amount of ECUs issued by the EMCF rose to nearly 50 billion in April 1981, but later fell to ECU 38 billion in July 1982. It increased again to ECU 42 billion in December 1982 (Table 27). Since July 1979, the quantity of gold contributed has remained virtually unchanged, while, since October 1979, the amount of U.S. dollars has fallen. The valuation of U.S. dollars fluctuated according to developments in exchange markets, keeping the ECU equivalent of U.S. dollar contributions, on balance, unchanged. The key to the growth of ECUs was the rise in the price of gold. As the shares of gold and U.S. dollars in the reserves (and hence in the contributions) of EMS central banks differ significantly, the distribution of ECUs among them is strongly affected by changes in the valuation of these two assets.

In sum, under the present provisions, the creation and distribution of ECUs is, apart from changes in international reserves of EMS member countries, determined by three variables that are outside the control of the system: the price of gold, the exchange rate of the U.S. dollar, and the respective share of these two assets. "Under these circumstances, the quantity of ECUs created cannot be expected necessarily to be consistent with the aims of the system...."[25] Various proposals to stabilize the amount of ECUs created have been presented but are at this time not under active consideration.

The actual use of ECUs has been limited. In December 1981, the positive or negative net positions of central banks in ECUs (i.e., amounts above or below those received from the EMCF) reached less than 8 percent of

---
[25] *European Economy*, No. 12 (July 1982), p. 44.

the amount of ECUs created through the swap arrangements; this percentage rose in the first half of 1982, before declining to around 7 percent in August 1982. A number of reasons may account for this development. Debtor central banks may have been reluctant to use ECUs, because the transitional character of the EMS could eventually require them to clear negative ECU positions by acquiring ECUs from other participants. On the other hand, creditor central banks may have discouraged the use of the ECU in view of its limited attractiveness, largely due to the lack of convertibility and the constraints on usability even within the system.

Credit Facilities

The very short-term financing facility has already been discussed. While this facility is limited to participants in the exchange rate mechanism, other EC credit facilities are open to all member countries, and their establishment preceded the coming into existence of the EMS. The short-term monetary support, which is administered by the EC central banks, is designed to provide finance for temporary balance of payments deficits on the request of a debtor central bank within the limits of its debtor quota; credits beyond these amounts are discretionary. The granting of medium-term financial assistance in the case of balance of payments difficulties is subject to a decision by the EC Council of Ministers which lays down economic policy conditions.

Another facility for dealing with balance of payments difficulties, the Community loan mechanism, is also of a medium-term nature and was established in 1975 in connection with the first round of oil price increases. Under this facility, the Community can borrow in the market or from other sources and on-lend to member countries up to ECU 6 billion.[26] As under the medium-term financial assistance facility, credits are subject to a Council decision and linked to economic policy conditions.

The usability of the short-term monetary support and medium-term financial assistance facilities, which are schemes of mutual assistance, depends on the strength of the balance of payments and reserve position of the EC as a whole. The Community loan mechanism, with its reliance on outside sources of finance, not only supplements but to a certain degree also substitutes for the other credit facilities, in particular the medium-term financial assistance facility. Apart from the very short-term financing facility, none of the credit facilities has been used since the start of the EMS. This may be explained by the relatively large reserves that at least some of the EMS countries have at their disposal. The easy access of EC countries to international markets may have made recourse to conditional credit facilities of the EC (or of the International Monetary Fund for that matter) less attractive, while the good credit rating of EC countries on the market may have been enhanced by the very existence of large credit facilities within the EC.

Proposals for Institutional Changes

In the European Council's Resolution of December 5, 1978, which laid down the framework for the "initial phase" of the EMS, the intention stated was "to consolidate, not later than two years after the start of the scheme, into a final system the provisions and procedures" of the initial phase.[27] In this second phase the EMS would "entail the creation of the European Monetary Fund [which would replace the European Monetary Cooperation Fund]... as well as the full utilization of the ECU as a reserve asset and a means of settlement."[28] The existing credit facilities were to be consolidated into a single fund.

Work on the next phase began soon after the start of the EMS in the Committee of Central Bank Governors and the Monetary Committee. The discussions concentrated on the following problems:

—The place and development of the ECU in the EMS. Of particular interest were the problems relating to a permanent transfer to the European Monetary Fund (EMF) of a certain portion of member countries' reserves against ECUs (compared with the provisional transfer on the basis of revolving swap arrangements as practiced at present); and to the role of the ECU as a means of settlement and its attractiveness as a reserve asset, with emphasis on such questions as full usability within the system and convertibility into other reserve assets.

—The credit mechanisms and their consolidation in the EMF. A special issue was the fact that the various credit facilities (the very short-term financing facility, the short-term monetary support, and the medium-term financial assistance facility) are subject to different procedures governing their use. They have different maturities and objectives and may or may not involve conditionality. Credits are to be granted under the responsibility of different institutions, the central banks in the case of the very short-term financing facility and the short-term monetary support, and the Council of Ministers in the case of the medium-term financial assistance facility.

—The role and structure of the EMF. The main questions were whether and to what degree the EMF should be autonomous from governments, and how

---

[26] On December 30, 1982, equivalent to SDR 5.25 billion.

[27] *European Economy*, No. 3 (July 1979), p. 95.
[28] Ibid.

III • THE EVOLUTION OF THE SYSTEM

its decision-making bodies would be composed; and what tasks and powers in the field of foreign exchange market intervention, granting of credits, and the creation of liquidity it should get.

Due in part to the worsening of the economic climate in the EC countries and the world at large, but mainly because of significant differences of opinion as to how these questions should be approached, the aim of limiting the initial, transitional phase to two years could not be observed. It became obvious that the economic, political, and legal problems would be formidable, going in scope far beyond technical considerations. Subsequently, a more gradual approach emerged, and, in early 1982, the EC Commission submitted to the Council of Ministers a set of proposals.[29] These proposals were intended to further the step-by-step development of the EMS in certain key areas without waiting for a final, fully developed system, and dealt with the following problems:

— method of issue of ECUs, with the aim of limiting the volatility in the amount of created ECUs;
— abolition of the acceptance limit (now 50 percent) for the use of ECUs in intra-EMS settlement of intervention debts;
— increased private use of ECUs;
— automaticity for financing of intramarginal intervention (i.e., in EMS currencies);
— measures to advance convergence, mainly by way of consultation and recommendation; and
— coordination of attitude toward third currencies, in particular the U.S. dollar.

By their very nature, these proposals concentrated on certain operational and technical aspects which can more easily be formalized but nevertheless might have important policy implications (e.g., acceptance limit for ECUs, financing of intramarginal intervention), whereas they were less specific in other areas, such as the promotion of convergence in economic performance or the coordination of attitude toward third currencies. After thorough discussions in the competent bodies of the EC, no agreement on the package of proposals could be reached. Some member countries who favored the proposals concentrated on their operational aspects and emphasized that their implementation would help to consolidate and strengthen the system by enhancing its predictability. Other member countries opposed the proposals on the grounds that their acceptance would have adverse implications for the conduct of domestic monetary policy. They stressed the need to keep the system flexible; as long as there was no sufficient degree of convergence of economic performance, any attempt to make the features of the system more stringent would only weaken and ultimately endanger the system. There was a general consensus that one of the prime objectives for the countries participating in the EMS remained the pursuit of policies conducive to greater convergence in economic performance.

---
[29] For the full text of the proposals, see *European Economy*, No. 12 (July 1982), Annex D, pp. 88–91.

IV. The European Monetary System and the International Monetary Fund

In its Resolution of December 5, 1978, the European Council stated: "The EMS is and will remain fully compatible with the relevant articles of the IMF Agreement."[30] At the time of the establishment of the EMS, however, a number of questions were raised as to whether the operations of the EMS might impede the Fund in carrying out its functions in accordance with the Articles of Agreement. Questions were asked as to whether the Fund's and the EMS's approaches to the same problems might differ and whether conflicts might arise. These doubts concentrated on three areas: surveillance over exchange rate policies, conditionality in credit operations, and the creation of international liquidity.

While it may be too early to come to a final assessment, the experience of the first years with EMS operations allows some observations and conclusions. At the outset, it may be said that any clear incompatibility of goals or of general policy orientation would have been surprising, taking into account that in the economic field the objectives of the Fund, as laid down in its Articles of Agreement, and of the European Community, as established in the EEC Treaty, are often identical and certainly consistent. It should be noted, however, that while the Fund's final objectives are of an economic nature, the EC, and with it the EMS, has ultimately a political purpose. The creation of the European Economic Community aspired, according to the Preamble of the Treaty, "to lay the foundations of an ever closer union among the peoples of Europe."[31] The EMS, in particular, is often viewed as preparing the ground for an eventual economic and monetary union by providing a high degree of exchange rate stability and a convergence of economic performance. While it is widely acknowledged that, during the first years of its existence, the EMS fell substantially short of some of its objectives, its ultimately political goals need to be kept in mind in judging policies and developments within the EMS.

Surveillance over Exchange Rate Policies

As described above, there have been several realignments of exchange rates in the EMS since its inception. While, in the beginning, exchange rate changes were apparently made without major controversy and, on the whole, in a smooth and timely fashion, more recent realignments led to discussions as to the direction and the size of adjustments "which became intense and at times difficult before unanimous consensus could be reached on a balanced rearrangement of the parity grid."[32] It should be recalled in this connection that exchange rate changes in the EMS are a matter of common decision making and require unanimity among EMS participants. This requirement is not surprising when one considers the importance of such decisions for the functioning of the EMS and for the achievement of its twin objectives, external and internal stability, and also bearing in mind other aspects of common EC policies.

The International Monetary Fund is not formally a partner in this decision-making process, and the formal obligations of EMS countries, in keeping with the bilateral nature of Fund-member relations, have been fully met by notifying the Fund promptly of any changes in exchange rate policies. It is obvious that the Fund and the EMS have a similarly strong interest in the effectiveness of exchange rates in facilitating international transactions and of securing international balance. There can always be differences in judgment regarding the timing of a decision, the magnitude of the exchange rate adjustment, and the appropriate mix of external and domestic measures. Such differences could arise from different weights placed on economic or other considerations and from different assessments of the impact of alternative policy adjustments. Recognition of such differences is implicit in the exercise of Fund surveillance over the exchange rate policies of its members, in which the Fund is required to respect the domestic social and political policies of members and to pay due regard

---
[30] *European Economy*, No. 3 (July 1979), p. 96.
[31] European Communities, *Treaties Establishing the European Communities: Treaties Amending These Treaties; Documents Concerning the Accession* (Luxembourg, 1973), p. 173.

[32] *European Economy*, No. 12 (July 1982), pp. 35–36.

to the circumstances of members.[33] In recent years, a number of European countries have tended to stress steadiness in exchange rate policy as a factor in the sociopolitical processes which influence present and future economic developments. A case in point is the "hard currency" option which emphasizes the importance of a stable nominal exchange rate for maintaining a high degree of domestic price stability which, in turn, is expected to influence favorably the social climate and, as a consequence, wage and cost developments. The EMS also needs to take into account other elements of common EC policies. It must look at adjustment policies also in the light of the quest for convergence as a way toward closer economic and monetary union.

Decisions on exchange rates are taken by national governments and the Fund's responsibility is to ensure that decisions taken (or not taken) by its member countries are appropriate given the interest of the international community. If there were serious doubts about the appropriateness of a particular decision, then the Fund would have a right and duty to question it.

Conditionality in Credit Operations

The question at issue is the desirability, indeed the need, to synchronize conditions in simultaneous or sequential borrowing operations by an EC country[34] from the Fund and under the various EC credit facilities. While in a strict sense this need would only refer to the use of the EC medium-term facilities (the medium-term financial assistance and Community loan facilities), use of the unconditional short-term monetary support scheme is also of interest since such short-term borrowing could later lead to consolidation under one of the medium-term facilities.

It can be assumed that any borrowing by an EC member country from the Fund or from an EC facility would have the same objective, namely, to give a country time to bring its balance of payments back in order. Again, as for other countries, differences may arise as to the nature of the adjustment policies to be implemented, perhaps in this case reflecting constraints related to common EC policies. However, such differences would be consistent with the Fund's obligation to pay due regard to the social and political objectives, the economic priorities, and the circumstances of members, provided the measures taken are adequate.[35]

The EC credit facilities (apart from the very short-term financing facility) have been used infrequently and not at all since the start of the EMS. Consequently, no distinct pattern for the decision-making process and the character of conditionality has developed within the EC. However, in connection with a change in the provisions governing the Community loan mechanism in March 1981, the procedures to be followed were more precisely defined. These procedures are very much in line with the Fund's policy as regards conditionality. Thus, the EC approach, called "graduation of conditionality,"[36] contains the elements of performance criteria, intermediate reviews, and the phasing of disbursements subject to compliance with the objectives of a stabilization program. Due to the limited number of its members and the special structure of its institutions, the decision-making process of the EC differs in character from that of the Fund. Regarding the medium-term facilities, the Council of Ministers, representing all EC countries, will determine whether a loan will be granted, the amount of a loan, and the economic policy conditions. The decisions of the Council will be prepared by the EC Commission and the EC Monetary Committee, which consists of high government and central bank officials and representatives of the Commission. In this way, from the beginning, all member governments, as well as the Commission, will be actively involved in designing and negotiating the framework for balance of payments assistance.

In its report on this subject[37] the Monetary Committee also states that no a priori position should be taken as to whether a country in need of balance of payments assistance should first use the one or the other medium-term EC facility or should seek assistance from the International Monetary Fund. Rather, the ranking of calls on the various sources of financing should depend on the circumstances at a given time.

Creation of International Liquidity

When the European Monetary System was being established, the question was raised of whether any capacity of the EMS to create international liquidity on its own would not diminish the interest of EMS countries in the creation of international liquidity, conditional or unconditional, by the IMF. It should be pointed out, however, that any international liquidity created by the EMS would not be "global" but "regional" in character. Any excess creation of such liquidity by the EMS would, over time, inevitably undermine the payments situation of the EMS, very much as the creation of excess national liquidity will erode a currency's international strength.

---

[33] Article IV, Section 3(*b*), Articles of Agreement of the International Monetary Fund (Washington, D.C., 1978).

[34] As mentioned earlier, the short-term monetary support and the medium-term financial assistance facilities, as well as the Community loan mechanism, can be used not only by those countries who actively participate in the EMS but also by the other EC member countries, that is, Greece and the United Kingdom.

[35] Decision No. 6056-(79/38), March 2, 1979, *Selected Decisions of the International Monetary Fund and Selected Documents*, Ninth Issue (Washington, June 15, 1981), p. 20.

[36] The Twenty-Second Report on the Activities of the Monetary Committee, *Official Journal of the European Communities*, C 124, Vol. 24 (May 25, 1981), p. 14.

[37] Ibid., pp. 12–19.

The creation of ECUs against the contribution of 20 percent of a country's gold and gross U.S. dollar reserves to the EMCF does not in itself constitute the creation of international liquidity. It only substitutes globally usable liquidity (U.S. dollars and gold) for liquidity that, at present, can only be used regionally and is subject to special restrictions.

While the creation of ECUs against gold does not create liquidity, it mobilizes reserves that otherwise may not have been used, and in this way may encourage less stringent policies. Because of the differences between the valuation of gold in the books of some EMS central banks and the market-related rates at which it is exchanged against ECUs, there is a statistical increase in international liquidity as shown in *International Financial Statistics*,[38] though this does not change the real liquidity position of a country. However, some of the central banks concerned employ procedures under which the domestic liquidity effect of such differences in gold valuation is sterilized.

The use of the EC and EMS credit facilities does not necessarily create international liquidity. For a credit under the very short-term financing facility, the amount of the creditor central bank's currency in circulation increases, and a debtor position in ECUs is created. While the debtor position will disappear with settlement of the debt, the question of whether the newly created amount of the creditor currency remains in circulation or will disappear depends on the means the debtor central bank will employ to meet its settlement obligations. If, under a credit facility like the short-term monetary support or the medium-term financial assistance, a credit was granted in EMS currencies, the effect would be similar to a transaction under the very short-term financing facility. If it was granted in foreign exchange (U.S. dollars) or in ECUs, there would only be a transfer of international liquidity from one central bank to another. A temporary creation of international liquidity could be imagined if the creditor central banks were to regard the claims they acquired as liquid, similar to a reserve tranche position in the IMF.

If, in the future, a European Monetary Fund were to be empowered to grant credits, the situation would be somewhat but not greatly changed. The granting of credits by a European Monetary Fund in ECUs would imply the replacement of national liquidity sources by an EC source. Presumably, the debtor central bank would convert ECUs with creditor central banks into national currencies or foreign exchange for intervention purposes, or use them outright for meeting settlement obligations. The effects in each case would be the same as in similar transactions described earlier, although with one important difference. Instead of claims on other central banks as at present, the creditor banks would receive newly issued ECUs, which are indistinguishable from other ECU holdings. In this way, there would be a temporary increase in international liquidity to the extent that actual use was made of loans from a European Monetary Fund. In the longer term, credit operations by a European Monetary Fund could give rise to a varying but permanent outstanding amount of additional ECUs.

An altogether different situation would exist once a European Monetary Fund is empowered to issue ECUs, not only against contributions in gold and U.S. dollars and in connection with credit operations, but also against national currencies or simply without any counterpart, similar to the IMF's allocation of special drawing rights (SDRs). The ECUs thus created would be indistinguishable from others and could be used in the same manner for settling intervention debts (or for any other international transaction that might be possible by then), and thus would contribute to an increase in international liquidity.

In this connection, it is interesting to examine whether the attitudes of EMS member countries on matters of monetary and liquidity policies have differed as they arose in the context of the IMF, the EMS, or in a strictly national framework. A careful look at individual EC member countries that participate in the EMS reveals that they attempt to adopt a consistent approach on monetary policy both in an international or national context. There are countries that follow a more conservative stability-oriented line in domestic monetary policy, with regard to liquidity creation within the EMS as well as with regard to the size of quota increases or the creation of SDRs in the IMF. And there are others that have adopted a less conservative and more expansion-oriented policy stance regarding domestic and international monetary problems.

To sum up, the European Monetary System does not at present permanently create international liquidity, except in a statistical sense. Schemes that could lead to the permanent creation of international liquidity, although only of a somewhat limited usability, will probably not be realized for some time to come. The present attitude of EMS member countries with regard to monetary policy does not give reason to assume that they would adopt different standards for monetary policy depending on whether they arise in the context of the International Monetary Fund or the European Monetary System.

---

[38] A monthly publication of the International Monetary Fund.

Appendix I
Statistical Tables

Table 1. EMS: Periods of Strain[1,2]

No.	Period	Source of Strain	Signaled by Divergence indicator	Signaled by Parity grid	Remedies Adopted
1	May-June 1979	D: Widening CA deficits and deficient capital inflow. B: Continued lack of confidence.	DKr: −75	DM/BF	Intervention to support both BF and DKr. B: Discount rate up from 6 to 9 percent. D: Discount rate up from 8 to 9 percent.
2	Aug.-Sept. 1979	D and B: Capital inflows induced by earlier increases in nominal interest rates dry out in both countries.	DKr: −75 BF: −75	DM/DKr	Intervention to support both BF and DKr. D: Discount rate up from 9 to 11 percent on Sept. 17 after which date intervention stops. B: Discount rate up from 9 to 10 percent. Realignment I: DM up, DKr down relative to other EMS currencies.
3	Nov. 1979	Uncertainty after parliamentary election in late October puts pressure on the DKr.	DKr: slightly negative few days before realignment		Intervention in support of DKr. Realignment II: DKr devalued against all other EMS currencies.
4	Dec. 1979-March 1980	D: Deficient capital inflow because of uncertainty about DKr in view of two recent realignments and because of increasing international nominal interest rates. B: Deficient capital inflow to finance CA deficits.		FF/BF (in March)	Intervention keeps DKr in the middle of the band. Discount rate up from 11 to 13 percent. B: Intervention majority in EMS currencies to support BF. Discount rate up from 10 to 14 percent.
5	Oct. 1980	G: Weak CA position relative to U.S. and major EMS countries plus interest differential disfavoring DM denominated investments.	DM: −70	FF/DM	Intervention in support of DM. F: Loosening of credit market. G: Slight tightening of credit market.
6	Feb. 1981	G: As U.S. interest rates surge and uncertainty about G's strategic (Poland) and economic position increases, pressure on DM becomes heavy.	DM: −60's FF: touching +75 occasionally in Jan. and Feb.	FF/BF and FF/DM	Intervention in $ and FF to support DM. G: Special Lombard rate introduced; substantial tightening of monetary policy.
7	March 1981	BF and Lit exposed at bottom of band subsequent to DM firming. After devaluation of Lit, BF remains under heavy pressure.	BF: −75 Lit: −75 (briefly)	DM/BF and FF/BF	I: Intervention followed by increase in discount rate from 16.5 to 19 percent. Realignment III: Devaluation of Lit. B: Intervention followed by increase in the discount rate from 12 to 16 percent.
8	May 1981	Presidential election in France (5/10/81).	FF: −75 (two weeks from 5/11/81)	DM/FF	F: Intervention. Interest rate and exchange control measures.
9	Aug.-Sept. 1981	On the background of pessimism as to the devaluation of the FF, DM gains strength on improving external performance, and FF and BF have problems following DM up against $.	DM: +75 (last two weeks of Sept.). BF: not past −75 but most "diverging" of weak currencies	DM/BF	Intervention in support of weak EMS currencies. Realignment IV: DM and f. revalued and FF and Lit devalued against DKr, BF, £Ir.
10	Nov. 1981	Brief pressure on BF when negotiations to form a government break down.	BF: once below −75 on Dec. 10		Intervention in support of BF. B: Discount rate from 13 to 15 percent.
11	Feb. 1982	Diminishing confidence in the future performance of the Belgian economy.	BF: close to, but not past −75. DKr: slightly negative		B: Intervention. Realignment V: Devaluation of BF and DKr against other EMS currencies.
12	March 1982	F: Widening inflation differential with G. DKr and BF lose strength acquired in previous realignments.	FF: one flash (−76) on March 23; otherwise well within bounds	DM/FF and f./FF	F: Intervention, tightening of monetary policy, exchange controls, budget tightening.
13	May-June 1982	"The weekend syndrome": pressure on BF, FF, Lit, especially late in week. Persistent realignment rumors.	DM: above +75 from end-April. BF: most "diverging" currency at bottom	DM/BF	Intervention. Realignment VI: Revaluation of DM and f. and devaluation of Lit and FF against DKr, BF, and £Ir.
14	Dec. 1982-March 1983	Deteriorating trade balance and inflation in France. Increasing pressure on FF, especially late in week; persistent realignment rumors; anticipation of realignment after March elections in Federal Republic of Germany, France.	BF: frequently below in January, February; FF: below in March	DM/FF f./BF	Substantial intervention in support of BF and FF, interest rate measures in Belgium, Federal Republic of Germany, Netherlands. Emergency foreign exchange measures in Belgium. Realignment VII: Revaluation of DM, f., DKr, BF, and devaluation of FF, Lit, £Ir.

Source: Fund staff estimates and calculations.
[1] Defined as periods with reports of substantial interference in the exchange market by intervention, capital and exchange controls, or measures of monetary policy motivated by exchange rate developments.
[2] Notation: B—Belgium; BF—Belgian franc; D—Denmark; DKr—Danish krone; F—France; FF—French franc; G—Federal Republic of Germany; DM—deutsche mark; £Ir—Irish pound; I—Italy; Lit—Italian lira; N—Netherlands; f.—Netherlands guilder; U.S.—United States; $—U.S. dollar; CA—current account.

Table 2. EMS: Bilateral Central Rates[1]

Currency Units	100 Belgian/ Luxembourg francs	100 Danish kroner	100 Deutsche mark	100 French francs	100 Italian lire	100 Irish pounds	100 Netherlands guilders
Belgian/Luxembourg francs							
Mar. 13, 1979		556.852	1,571.64	680.512	3.43668	5,954.71	1,450.26
Sept. 24, 1979		540.942	1,603.07	680.512	3.43668	5,954.71	1,450.26
Nov. 30, 1979		515.186	1,603.07	680.512	3.43668	5,954.71	1,450.26
March 23, 1981		515.186	1,603.07	680.512	3.23048	5,954.71	1,450.26
Oct. 5, 1981		515.186	1,691.25	660.097	3.13355	5,954.71	1,530.03
Feb. 22, 1982		546.154	1,848.37	721.415	3.42466	6,507.92	1,672.16
June 14, 1982		546.154	1,926.93	679.941	3.33047	6,507.92	1,743.23
March 21, 1983		551.536	2,002.85	653.144	3.19922	6,187.32	1,777.58
Danish kroner							
Mar. 13, 1979	17.9581		282.237	122.207	0.617161	1,069.35	260.439
Sept. 24, 1979	18.4862		296.348	125.801	0.635312	1,100.81	268.098
Nov. 30, 1979	19.4105		311.165	132.091	0.667078	1,155.84	281.503
Mar. 23, 1981	19.4105		311.165	132.091	0.627052	1,155.84	281.503
Oct. 5, 1981	19.4105		328.279	128.128	0.60824	1,155.84	296.986
Feb. 22, 1982	18.3098		338.433	132.09	0.62705	1,191.59	306.171
June 14, 1982	18.3098		352.817	124.496	0.609804	1,191.59	319.183
Mar. 21, 1983	18.1312		363.141	118.423	0.580057	1,121.84	322.297
Deutsche mark							
Mar. 13, 1979	6.36277	35.4313		43.2995	0.218668	378.886	92.2767
Sept. 24, 1979	6.238	33.7441		42.4505	0.21438	371.457	90.4673
Nov. 30, 1979	6.238	32.1373		42.4505	0.21438	371.457	90.4673
Mar. 23, 1981	6.238	32.1373		42.4505	0.201518	371.457	90.4673
Oct. 5, 1981	5.9128	30.4619		39.0302	0.185281	352.09	90.4673
Feb. 22, 1982	5.41018	29.5479		39.0302	0.185281	352.090	90.4673
June 14, 1982	5.18961	28.3433		35.2863	0.172839	337.736	90.4673
Mar. 21, 1983	4.99288	27.5375		32.6107	0.159733	308.925	88.7526
French francs							
Mar. 13, 1979	14.6948	81.8286	230.95		0.505013	875.034	213.113
Sept. 24, 1979	14.6948	79.4905	235.568		0.505013	875.034	213.113
Nov. 30, 1979	14.6948	75.7054	235.568		0.505013	875.034	213.113
Mar. 23, 1981	14.6948	75.7054	235.568		0.474714	875.034	213.113
Oct. 5, 1981	15.1493	78.047	256.212		0.474714	902.098	231.789
Feb. 22, 1982	13.8616	75.706	256.212		0.474714	902.098	231.789
June 14, 1982	14.7072	80.3239	283.396		0.489818	957.129	256.38
Mar. 21, 1983	15.3106	84.4432	306.648		0.489819	947.313	272.158
Italian lire							
Mar. 13, 1979	2,909.79	16,303.3	45,731.4	19,801.5		173,270.0	42,199.5
Sept. 24, 1979	2,909.79	15,740.3	46,646.0	19,801.5		173,270.0	42,199.5
Nov. 30, 1979	2,909.79	14,990.7	46,646.0	19,801.5		173,270.0	42,199.5
Mar. 23, 1981	3,095.51	15,947.6	49,623.2	21,065.3		184,329.0	44,893.0
Oct. 5, 1981	3,191.26	16,440.9	53,972.2	21,065.3		190,031.0	48,827.2
Feb. 22, 1982	2,920.0	15,947.70	53,972.2	21,065.3		190,031.0	48,827.2
June 14, 1982	3,002.58	16,398.7	57,857.4	20,415.7		195,405.0	52,341.9
Mar. 21, 1983	3,125.76	17,239.7	62,604.3	20,415.7		193,401.0	55,563.0
Irish pounds							
Mar. 13, 1979	1.67934	9.35146	26.3932	11.4281	0.0577136		24.3548
Sept. 24, 1979	1.67934	9.08424	26.921	11.4281	0.0577136		24.3548
Nov. 30, 1979	1.67934	8.65169	26.921	11.4281	0.0577136		24.3548
Mar. 23, 1981	1.67934	8.65169	26.921	11.4281	0.0542508		24.3548
Oct. 5, 1981	1.67934	8.65169	28.4018	11.0853	0.052623		25.6944
Feb. 22, 1982	1.53659	8.39216	28.4018	11.0853	0.052623		25.6944
June 14, 1982	1.53659	8.39216	29.6090	10.4479	0.05111758		26.7864
Mar. 21, 1983	1.61621	8.91396	32.3703	10.5562	0.0517061		28.7295
Netherlands guilders							
Mar. 13, 1979	6.89531	38.3967	108.37	46.9235	0.23697	410.597	
Sept. 24, 1979	6.89531	37.2998	110.537	46.9235	0.23697	410.597	
Nov. 30, 1979	6.89531	35.5237	110.537	46.9235	0.23697	410.597	
Mar. 23, 1981	6.89531	35.5237	110.537	46.9235	0.222752	410.597	
Oct. 5, 1981	6.53583	33.6716	110.537	43.1428	0.204804	389.19	
Feb. 22, 1982	5.98027	32.6615	110.537	43.1428	0.204804	389.190	
June 14, 1982	5.73646	31.3300	110.537	39.0045	0.191051	373.324	
Mar. 21, 1983	5.62561	31.0273	112.673	36.7434	0.179976	348.075	

Sources: Commission of the European Communities; and Fund staff calculations.

[1] Expressed as the price of 100 units of the currency on top of the column in the currency in front of the row.

Table 3. EMS Realignments: Percentage Changes in Bilateral Central Rates[1]

	Sept. 24, 1979	Nov. 30, 1979	Mar. 23, 1981	Oct. 5, 1981	Feb. 22, 1982	June 14, 1982	Mar. 21, 1983
Belgian and Luxembourg francs					−8.5		+1.5
Danish krone	−2.9	−4.8			−3.0		+2.5
Deutsche mark	+2.0			+5.5		+4.25	+5.5
French franc				−3.0		−5.75	−2.5
Italian lira			−6.0	−3.0		−2.75	−2.5
Irish pound							−3.5
Netherlands guilder				+5.5		+4.25	+3.5

Sources: Commission of the European Communities; and Fund staff calculations.

[1] Calculated as the percentage change against the group of currencies whose bilateral parities remained unchanged in the realignment, except for the most recent realignment (3/21/83) in which all currencies were realigned—for this the percentages are shown as in the official communiqué.

Table 4. EMS: ECU Central Rates[1]

	Mar. 13, 1979	Sept. 24, 1979	Nov. 30, 1979	Mar. 23, 1981	Oct. 5, 1981	Feb. 22, 1982	June 14, 1982	Mar. 21, 1983
Belgian/Luxembourg franc								
Units of national currency per ECU	39.4582	39.8456	39.7897	40.7985	40.7572	44.6963	44.9704	44.3662
Percentage change from previous central rate		0.98	−0.14	2.54	−0.10	9.66	0.61	−1.34
Percentage change from initial central rate		0.98	0.84	3.40	3.29	13.28	13.97	12.44
Danish krone								
Units of national currency per ECU	7.08592	7.36594	7.72336	7.91917	7.91117	8.18382	8.2340	8.04412
Percentage change from previous central rate		3.95	4.85	2.54	−0.10	3.45	0.61	−2.31
Percentage change from initial central rate		3.95	9.00	11.76	11.65	15.49	16.20	13.52
Deutsche mark								
Units of national currency per ECU	2.51064	2.48557	2.48208	2.54502	2.40989	2.41815	2.33379	2.21515
Percentage change from previous central rate		−1.00	−0.1	2.54	−5.31	0.34	−3.48	−5.08
Percentage change from initial central rate		−1.00	−0.1	1.37	−4.01	−3.68	−7.04	−11.77
French franc								
Units of national currency per ECU	5.79831	5.85522	5.84700	5.99526	6.17443	6.19564	6.61387	6.79271
Percentage change from previous central rate		0.98	−0.14	2.54	2.99	0.34	6.75	2.70
Percentage change from initial central rate		0.98	0.84	3.40	6.49	6.85	14.07	17.15
Italian lira								
Units of national currency per ECU	1,148.15	1,159.42	1,157.79	1,262.92	1,300.67	1,305.13	1,350.27	1,386.78
Percentage change from previous central rate		0.98	−0.14	9.1	2.99	0.34	3.46	2.70
Percentage change from initial central rate		0.98	0.84	10.00	13.28	13.67	17.60	20.78
Irish pound								
Units of national currency per ECU	0.662638	0.669141	0.668201	0.685145	0.684452	0.686799	0.691011	0.71705
Percentage change from previous central rate		0.98	−0.14	2.54	−0.10	0.34	0.61	3.77
Percentage change from initial central rate		0.98	0.84	3.40	3.29	3.65	4.28	8.21
Netherlands guilder								
Units of national currency per ECU	2.72077	2.74748	2.74362	2.81318	2.66382	2.67296	2.57971	2.49587
Percentage change from previous central rate		0.98	−0.14	2.54	−5.31	0.34	−3.49	−3.25
Percentage change from initial central rate		0.98	0.84	3.40	−2.09	−1.76	−5.18	−8.27

Source: Commission of the European Communities.

[1] The change of any central rate expressed in terms of ECUs implies a simultaneous change of all other ECU central rates, since the ECU is made up of a basket of currencies. Positive sign indicates depreciation relative to the ECU.

APPENDIX I • STATISTICAL TABLES

Table 5. EMS: Interest Differentials for Three-Month Deposits, 1979–82[1]

		Belgium[2] Uncovered[3]	Covered[3,4]	France Uncovered[3]	Covered[3,4]	Fed. Rep. of Germany Uncovered[3]	Covered[3,4]	Italy Uncovered[3]	Covered[3,4]	Netherlands Uncovered[3]	Covered[3,4]
1979	Mar.	2.83	−0.50	3.56	0.87	5.33	−0.53	−1.06	−0.24	3.50	−0.29
	Apr.	2.51	−0.48	3.88	1.21	5.23	−0.72	−0.68	0.31	3.44	−0.02
	May	1.79	0.62	2.07	3.03	4.54	−0.28	−0.62	1.98	1.69	0.06
	June	0.88	0.79	1.38	2.06	4.08	−0.28	−0.81	1.99	2.25	−0.05
	July	−0.62	0.02	0.76	1.67	4.53	−0.53	−0.18	4.56	1.88	−0.30
	Aug.	−0.19	−0.04	0.81	1.25	4.79	−0.12	0.63	3.15	2.63	−0.27
	Sept.	−0.03	0.53	1.12	1.85	4.80	−0.65	1.19	3.70	2.94	−0.40
	Oct.	1.28	−0.18	2.88	1.50	5.88	−0.95	2.26	3.89	5.00	−0.76
	Nov.	−0.35	−0.17	1.62	1.39	4.35	−1.08	0.50	2.66	−0.50	−1.12
	Dec.	0.43	−0.01	2.31	1.81	5.01	−1.08	−2.69	1.21	1.56	−0.66
1980	Jan.	−0.13	−0.37	2.13	0.48	5.53	−0.65	−3.31	3.03	3.07	−0.11
	Feb.	1.63	0.08	3.25	0.55	7.90	−0.14	−1.00	1.49	4.12	1.49
	Mar.	2.00	0.27	6.00	0.02	9.90	−0.70	1.63	−0.16	8.56	−0.16
	Apr.	−2.00	−1.10	1.38	0.03	4.08	−0.79	−1.93	0.04	4.57	0.16
	May.	−6.13	−0.75	−1.93	0.56	0.39	−0.23	−6.62	1.22	−0.62	0.35
	June	−5.19	−0.61	−2.44	0.15	−0.14	−0.47	−7.63	9.23	−0.69	0.09
	July	−2.44	−0.12	−1.56	0.37	0.69	−0.84	−7.56	5.39	0.57	0.08
	Aug.	−0.79	...	0.75	0.71	3.30	−0.60	−5.06	10.11	1.63	0.07
	Sept.	1.46	−0.08	1.69	0.19	4.91	−0.03	−4.57	5.57	3.94	0.07
	Oct.	2.49	−0.22	3.38	−0.35	6.18	−0.45	−2.37	2.95	6.13	0.01
	Nov.	4.81	−0.19	6.63	−0.40	8.30	−0.48	0.38	0.82	8.06	−0.26
	Dec.	4.34	−0.71	6.32	−0.20	7.62	−1.54	0.32	1.06	8.57	−0.45
1981	Jan.	6.09	−0.88	6.38	−0.41	8.03	−0.31	0.01	1.29	8.19	−0.27
	Feb.	3.56	0.35	2.81	0.05	2.05	−0.27	−0.88	0.88	5.38	−0.04
	Mar.	−2.12	2.94	1.83	0.85	1.31	−0.94	−3.38	1.40	4.63	−0.04
	Apr.	−0.12	1.30	3.26	0.28	3.82	−0.70	−2.94	−0.62	6.00	0.43
	May	2.46	1.63	−0.44	2.36	4.28	−1.07	−2.44	1.97	5.37	−0.45
	June	3.25	0.61	−0.12	4.84	4.72	−0.91	−2.87	3.48	6.01	−0.37
	July	2.19	5.46	1.51	4.38	5.66	−1.02	−2.13	7.68	5.38	−0.71
	Aug.	2.82	5.84	0.70	10.15	5.36	−0.76	−2.94	10.64	4.56	...
	Sept.	1.69	7.36	−0.88	8.60	5.46	−0.53	−3.37	11.52	5.01	−0.10
	Oct.	0.71	4.69	0.25	2.02	3.95	−0.52	−5.41	0.89	2.97	−0.11
	Nov.	−2.50	1.75	−3.91	0.41	1.16	−0.48	−9.32	−0.49	0.94	0.12
	Dec.	−1.94	3.86	−1.28	1.69	2.93	−0.38	−7.50	1.50	2.94	−0.03
1982	Jan.	0.63	4.90	−0.90	0.11	4.12	−0.38	−6.94	0.16	4.50	−0.14
	Feb.	0.63	0.65	0.87	1.72	4.67	−0.63	−5.82	0.09	5.44	−0.14
	Mar.	0.75	2.36	−0.78	8.85	5.71	−0.93	−5.31	5.00	7.07	−0.51
	April	−0.06	2.15	−1.86	5.95	5.62	−0.83	−5.75	3.29	6.44	−0.49
	May	−0.31	1.54	−1.85	9.07	5.19	−1.01	−6.25	2.67	5.75	−0.41
	June	0.63	0.88	0.73	2.01	6.36	−0.89	−4.56	1.18	6.88	−0.53
	July	−1.62	−0.41	−1.95	1.18	3.57	−0.91	−6.87	−0.08	4.07	−0.13
	Aug.	−3.34	−0.29	−2.75	7.44	3.07	−0.39	−7.31	1.81	3.63	0.08
	Sept.	−1.37	0.26	−2.57	3.88	3.29	−0.61	−7.13	0.22	3.56	−0.23
	Oct.	−2.60	0.14	−3.12	6.01	2.61	−0.42	−8.82	1.25	3.44	−0.05

Source: Fund staff calculations.
[1] End of month.
[2] Rates pertain to last Tuesday of the month.
[3] Positive sign indicates differential in favor of Eurodollar investment relative to domestic investment, while negative sign indicates the reverse. Domestic interest rates for France, the Federal Republic of Germany, Italy, and the Netherlands are interbank rates. For Belgium the rate on four-month certificates of the Government Securities Stabilization Fund is used.
[4] Covered interest differential is calculated as the uncovered interest differential minus the forward exchange quotation.

Table 6. EMS: Economic Measures in Connection with Realignments[1]

Realignment Date	Realignment Wording Based on Official Communiqué	Major Measures in Belgium	Major Measures in Denmark	Major Measures in France	Major Measures in Italy
September 24, 1979	Shift in cross-rate between DM and DKr of 5 percent. Shift in cross-rate between DM and other EMS currencies of 2 percent	—	—	—	—
November 30, 1979	Devaluation of DKr by 5 percent against other EMS currencies (no communiqué)	—	• Energy component removed from wage-regulating index • Short-term price and wage freeze measures • Increases in direct personal wealth and corporate taxes	—	—
March 23, 1981	Devaluation of Lit by 6 percent against other EMS currencies	—	—	—	• Discount rate up 2½ percent to 19 percent • Government spending cut plans
October 5, 1981	Revaluation of DM and f. by 5.5 percent against DKr, BF, Lux F, £Ir. Devaluation of FF, Lit by 3 percent against DKr, BF, £Ir	—	—	• Temporary price and profit freeze • Incomes policy aiming at maintenance of average income purchasing power, narrowing of income range • FF 10.15 billion government expenditure in suspense	—
February 22, 1982	Devaluation of BF, Lux F, by 8.5 percent and of DKr by 3 percent against other EMS currencies	• Temporary freeze of wages and longer-run measures to impede complete wage indexation • Temporary price freeze • Reduction in corporate tax burden • Measures to stimulate the stock market	—	—	—
June 14, 1982	Change in bilateral rates: between FF and DM, f.: 10 percent; between Lit and DM, f.: 7 percent; between DKr, BF, Lux F, £Ir and DM, f.: 4.25 percent	—	—	• Temporary freeze of wages, prices, rents and dividends (except minimum wage) to be followed up by agreements on price and dividend behavior and indexation practices for wages • Revision of 1983 budget to restrict deficit to FF 120 billion (3 percent of gross national product)	• Announcement of budgetary austerity measures, June 23.
March 21, 1983	Change in central rates: Deutsche mark +5.5 Netherlands guilder +3.5 Danish krone +2.5 Belgian franc +1.5 Luxembourg franc +1.5 French franc −2.5 Italian lira −2.5 Irish pound −3.5	—	—	• Package of restrictive measures in budgetary, monetary, and foreign exchange fields.	—

Sources: Commission of the European Communities and Fund staff.
[1] Notation: BF—Belgian franc; DKr—Danish krone; FF—French franc; DM—deutsche mark; £Ir—Irish pound; Lit—Italian lira; Lux F—Luxembourg franc f.—Netherlands guilder.

APPENDIX I · STATISTICAL TABLES

Table 7. Variability of Nominal Effective Exchange Rates, 1974–82[1,2]

	1974	1975	1976	1977	1978	Average 1974–78	1979	1980	1981	Average 1979–81	1982
Belgium	21.7	23.2	27.6	9.4	15.4	*19.5*	9.3	14.5	14.5	*12.8*	35.9
Denmark	26.6	18.5	24.8	18.0	14.4	*20.5*	17.4	20.1	24.3	*20.6*	19.5
France	27.9	21.9	40.3	5.4	17.1	*22.5*	14.6	18.3	31.5	*21.5*	40.8
Germany, Federal Republic of	25.9	23.6	36.5	20.2	20.4	*25.3*	23.0	23.9	22.4	*23.1*	15.9
Ireland	10.9	39.6	63.3	15.8	19.7	*29.9*	12.4	22.9	23.4	*19.6*	10.8
Italy	31.5	5.4	63.4	14.7	20.1	*27.0*	8.6	28.9	39.5	*25.7*	15.7
Netherlands	23.1	19.5	33.5	8.1	16.8	*20.2*	11.0	13.1	26.0	*16.7*	14.7
Average EMS[3]	**23.9**	**21.7**	**41.3**	**13.1**	**17.7**	**23.6**	**13.8**	**20.2**	**25.9**	**20.0**	**21.9**
Austria	33.6	21.4	31.8	17.2	14.2	*23.6*	32.9	22.5	23.9	*26.4*	10.0
Canada	6.9	15.1	16.2	9.4	39.5	*17.4*	14.3	7.2	17.3	*12.9*	19.8
Japan	31.2	10.0	21.6	53.7	85.5	*40.4*	70.9	70.3	21.4	*54.2*	35.1
Norway	20.0	25.6	26.6	21.5	23.1	*23.4*	8.8	7.4	10.3	*8.8*	44.1
Sweden	23.1	22.8	21.2	60.7	1.9	*25.9*	14.5	4.3	49.6	*22.8*	67.1
Switzerland	54.6	13.0	24.8	54.1	59.4	*41.2*	18.4	18.3	55.9	*30.9*	24.2
United Kingdom	11.0	41.8	71.6	12.7	26.1	*32.6*	40.2	30.1	58.3	*42.9*	20.0
United States	18.5	29.9	7.5	14.3	35.7	*21.2*	10.3	23.5	48.8	*27.5*	44.3
Average non-EMS[3]	**24.9**	**22.5**	**27.7**	**30.5**	**35.7**	**28.3**	**26.3**	**23.0**	**35.7**	**28.3**	**33.1**
Average European non-EMS[3]	28.5	24.9	35.2	33.2	24.9	*29.3*	23.0	16.5	39.6	*26.4*	33.1

Sources: International Monetary Fund, *International Financial Statistics*; and Fund staff calculations.
[1] Based on the IMF's multilateral exchange rate model (MERM) and monthly data.
[2] Variability is measured by the coefficient of variation (multiplied by 1,000) of monthly exchange rates.
[3] Unweighted average.

Table 8. Variability of Nominal Exchange Rates Against EMS Currencies, 1974–82[1]

	1974	1975	1976	1977	1978	Average 1974–78	1979	1980	1981	Average 1979–81	1982[2]
Belgium	21.3	17.8	34.5	12.2	15.8	*20.3*	8.1	6.2	17.0	*10.4*	37.8
Denmark	24.6	14.6	41.3	28.1	16.3	*25.0*	26.3	7.8	17.7	*17.3*	18.4
France	32.8	26.7	57.6	15.0	26.3	*31.7*	9.2	7.3	21.8	*12.8*	34.1
Germany, Federal Republic of	28.9	20.8	53.0	21.8	21.8	*29.3*	12.2	6.5	28.0	*15.6*	29.4
Ireland	26.5	33.4	73.2	16.6	30.1	*36.0*	12.1	6.9	15.5	*11.5*	22.0
Italy	41.8	18.7	70.3	20.4	28.7	*36.0*	14.1	11.5	27.9	*17.8*	18.6
Netherlands	21.8	15.0	39.4	13.2	16.0	*21.1*	9.3	7.5	22.8	*13.2*	22.9
Average EMS[3]	**28.2**	**21.0**	**52.8**	**18.2**	**22.1**	**28.5**	**13.0**	**7.7**	**21.5**	**14.1**	**26.2**
Austria	26.5	12.4	34.8	13.6	14.0	*20.3*	16.9	6.1	21.0	*14.7*	17.0
Canada	30.3	42.6	45.4	42.1	60.4	*44.2*	28.0	30.0	66.5	*41.5*	38.1
Japan	41.9	31.7	39.3	40.3	69.4	*44.5*	78.9	88.2	32.8	*66.6*	19.9
Norway	20.3	16.1	34.1	28.1	28.1	*25.3*	12.4	24.4	26.7	*21.1*	27.9
Sweden	19.9	14.9	33.7	65.6	17.1	*30.2*	13.7	22.4	48.7	*28.3*	19.3
Switzerland	45.8	21.5	45.0	49.0	59.0	*44.1*	9.8	17.1	65.7	*30.9*	24.4
United Kingdom	24.0	30.0	67.2	14.6	27.4	*32.6*	35.3	52.3	44.6	*44.1*	21.3
United States	32.5	44.5	38.5	19.1	38.7	*34.7*	23.0	40.9	71.2	*45.0*	47.9
Average non-EMS[3]	**30.2**	**26.7**	**42.3**	**34.1**	**39.3**	**34.5**	**27.2**	**35.2**	**47.2**	**36.5**	**27.0**
Average European non-EMS[3]	27.3	19.0	43.0	34.2	29.1	*30.5*	17.6	24.5	41.3	*27.8*	22.0

Sources: International Monetary Fund, *International Financial Statistics*; and Fund staff calculations.
[1] Weighted average (MERM weights) of variability of bilateral nominal exchange rate against EMS currencies, with variability measured by coefficient of variation (multiplied by 1,000) of bilateral exchange rates.
[2] First nine months only.
[3] Unweighted average.

Statistical Tables

Table 9. Variability of Nominal Exchange Rates Against Non-EMS Currencies, 1974–82[1]

	1974	1975	1976	1977	1978	Average 1974–78	1979	1980	1981	Average 1979–81	1982[2]
Belgium	36.6	40.8	29.4	31.1	45.7	*36.7*	33.8	43.9	53.1	*43.6*	52.3
Denmark	32.6	33.6	25.5	30.6	39.0	*32.3*	30.3	38.8	53.7	*40.9*	33.1
France	33.8	34.5	47.9	27.0	45.9	*37.8*	35.6	44.5	60.7	*46.9*	50.0
Germany, Federal Republic of	34.3	35.1	30.0	32.6	46.4	*35.7*	39.3	45.9	48.1	*44.4*	23.2
Ireland	18.1	47.5	61.4	25.7	32.3	*37.0*	29.1	43.4	65.0	*45.8*	27.5
Italy	24.8	28.7	70.6	26.3	39.9	*38.1*	32.0	53.9	57.8	*47.9*	28.5
Netherlands	35.3	38.9	35.4	28.8	45.7	*36.8*	32.5	40.6	57.6	*43.6*	24.1
Average EMS[3]	**30.8**	**37.0**	**42.9**	**28.9**	**42.1**	**36.3**	**33.2**	**44.4**	**56.6**	**44.7**	**34.1**
Austria	44.0	38.0	33.4	35.2	46.9	*39.5*	49.9	45.5	51.5	*49.0*	24.9
Canada	12.9	16.7	17.0	34.1	36.1	*23.4*	18.3	18.3	17.0	*17.9*	23.3
Japan	33.3	22.1	22.1	59.5	96.7	*46.7*	68.3	64.7	48.5	*60.5*	45.5
Norway	30.5	40.2	30.7	34.4	42.4	*35.6*	29.9	30.0	42.9	*34.3*	40.2
Sweden	33.4	37.3	25.8	64.3	38.7	*39.9*	30.6	28.2	65.5	*41.4*	25.7
Switzerland	63.1	28.1	18.7	57.4	72.8	*48.0*	38.1	43.0	62.1	*47.7*	29.3
United Kingdom	25.7	56.4	82.5	34.4	48.8	*49.6*	54.0	34.4	79.8	*56.1*	26.0
United States	24.3	24.7	22.2	41.3	58.2	*34.1*	37.2	38.2	40.5	*38.6*	36.8
Average non-EMS[3]	**33.4**	**32.9**	**31.5**	**45.1**	**55.1**	**39.6**	**40.8**	**37.8**	**51.0**	**43.2**	**31.5**
Average European non-EMS[3]	39.3	40.0	38.2	45.1	49.9	*42.5*	40.5	36.2	60.4	*45.7*	29.2

Sources: International Monetary Fund, *International Financial Statistics*; and Fund staff calculations.
[1] Weighted average (MERM weights) of variability, measured by coefficient of variation of bilateral nominal exchange rates against the eight non-EMS countries listed.
[2] First nine months only.
[3] Unweighted average.

Table 10. Variability of Bilateral Real Exchange Rates Against EMS Currencies, 1974–82[1]

	1974	1975	1976	1977	1978	Average 1974–78	1979	1980	1981	Average 1979–81	1982[2]
Belgium	31.8	19.3	31.4	8.5	19.0	*22.0*	17.2	14.0	10.7	*14.0*	37.6
Denmark	28.9	24.3	43.7	14.6	18.4	*26.0*	22.1	14.9	12.7	*16.6*	15.2
France	29.0	30.9	48.2	10.3	32.9	*30.3*	15.7	19.3	11.8	*15.6*	29.0
Germany, Federal Republic of	36.6	32.1	37.2	11.7	22.4	*28.0*	16.6	25.4	12.7	*18.2*	21.5
Ireland	25.4	29.3	46.1	11.8	25.4	*27.6*	22.1	16.8	15.6	*18.2*	11.2
Italy	24.8	25.0	48.5	11.0	21.4	*26.1*	22.8	23.8	12.3	*19.6*	17.0
Netherlands	22.6	19.9	35.7	11.3	16.3	*21.2*	19.2	14.7	15.3	*16.4*	16.1
Average EMS[3]	**28.4**	**25.8**	**41.5**	**11.3**	**22.3**	**25.9**	**19.4**	**18.4**	**13.0**	**16.9**	**21.1**
Austria	24.7	18.9	29.4	8.5	15.7	*19.4*	14.3	15.1	10.2	*13.2*	12.7
Canada	32.2	50.3	38.6	38.7	57.3	*43.4*	32.4	32.9	68.0	*44.4*	34.1
Japan	31.1	34.3	35.2	34.8	66.2	*40.3*	85.1	83.3	26.4	*64.9*	25.2
Norway	21.0	19.3	29.7	27.2	26.4	*24.7*	20.7	31.7	24.7	*25.7*	25.2
Sweden	21.6	18.8	28.5	52.9	18.9	*28.1*	14.5	29.5	53.3	*32.4*	15.1
Switzerland	38.1	23.5	32.7	36.2	47.8	*35.7*	19.3	18.0	52.7	*30.0*	22.8
United Kingdom	22.7	23.1	54.5	16.0	24.3	*28.1*	56.6	60.6	43.4	*53.5*	15.7
United States	34.4	45.4	30.9	21.6	32.9	*33.0*	21.2	43.9	69.3	*44.8*	43.3
Average non-EMS[3]	**28.2**	**29.2**	**34.9**	**29.5**	**36.2**	**31.6**	**33.0**	**39.4**	**43.5**	**38.6**	**24.3**
Average European non-EMS[3]	25.6	20.6	35.0	28.2	26.6	*27.2*	25.1	31.0	36.9	*31.0*	18.3

Sources: International Monetary Fund, *International Financial Statistics*; and Fund staff calculations.
[1] Weighted average (MERM weights) of the variability of bilateral real exchange rates (as measured by nominal exchange rates adjusted for relative consumer price movements) against EMS countries, with variability measured by the coefficient of variation (multiplied by 1,000) of the bilateral real exchange rate.
[2] First nine months only.
[3] Unweighted average.

APPENDIX I • STATISTICAL TABLES

Table 11. Variability of Bilateral Real Exchange Rates Against Non-EMS Currencies, 1974–82[1]

	1974	1975	1976	1977	1978	Average 1974–78	1979	1980	1981	Average 1979–81	1982[2]
Belgium	42.8	35.7	31.1	27.9	40.8	*35.7*	36.6	50.6	56.5	*47.9*	48.5
Denmark	38.7	41.5	38.7	28.9	38.3	*37.2*	35.2	40.9	50.0	*42.0*	28.8
France	34.4	31.1	38.6	27.2	44.8	*35.2*	41.2	41.9	52.5	*45.2*	42.0
Germany, Federal Republic of	29.1	43.3	24.3	27.8	38.6	*32.6*	35.8	58.9	50.2	*48.3*	23.8
Ireland	25.3	49.3	36.7	25.6	29.6	*33.3*	29.6	44.5	52.4	*42.2*	18.7
Italy	26.4	24.0	49.4	26.4	36.0	*32.5*	48.6	38.1	51.1	*45.9*	26.3
Netherlands	30.6	36.6	38.4	25.4	39.8	*34.2*	35.1	48.9	61.4	*48.5*	25.5
Average EMS[3]	**32.5**	**37.4**	**36.7**	**27.0**	**38.3**	**34.4**	**37.4**	**46.3**	**53.4**	**45.7**	**30.5**
Austria	35.0	42.7	30.4	29.6	39.2	*35.4*	43.3	56.5	55.2	*51.7*	26.0
Canada	13.9	14.9	17.2	26.5	36.5	*21.8*	22.7	18.3	22.1	*21.0*	20.0
Japan	30.6	21.4	28.1	52.6	84.9	*43.5*	84.6	57.0	59.7	*67.1*	51.9
Norway	23.2	36.6	28.5	30.3	39.3	*31.6*	36.9	29.8	52.4	*39.7*	31.6
Sweden	28.6	32.7	28.8	48.1	32.1	*34.1*	33.1	29.8	66.8	*43.2*	25.7
Switzerland	53.6	36.5	14.8	50.1	61.1	*43.2*	33.8	52.8	62.7	*49.8*	36.0
United Kingdom	30.0	30.5	62.6	33.3	43.0	*40.0*	77.2	36.5	69.8	*61.3*	26.2
United States	24.9	21.1	23.6	35.9	51.8	*31.5*	46.5	36.7	47.1	*43.4*	36.9
Average non-EMS[3]	**30.0**	**30.0**	**29.3**	**38.3**	**48.5**	**35.1**	**47.1**	**39.7**	**54.5**	**47.1**	**31.8**
Average European non-EMS[3]	34.1	35.8	33.0	38.3	42.9	*36.8*	44.7	42.5	60.3	*49.1*	29.1

Sources: International Monetary Fund, *International Financial Statistics*; and Fund staff calculations.
[1] Weighted average (MERM weights) of variability of bilateral real exchange rates against the above eight non-EMS countries as a group, with variability measured by the coefficient of variation (multiplied by 1,000) of the bilateral real exchange rate.
[2] First nine months only.
[3] Unweighted average.

Table 12. Consumer Price Indices, 1974–82

(Annual change in percent)

	1974	1975	1976	1977	1978	Average[1] 1974–78	1979	1980	1981	Average[1] 1979–81	1982[2]
Belgium	12.7	12.7	9.2	7.1	4.5	*9.2*	4.5	6.6	7.6	*6.2*	9.0
Denmark	15.2	9.6	9.0	11.1	10.0	*11.0*	9.6	12.3	11.7	*11.2*	10.0
France	13.7	11.8	9.6	9.4	9.1	*10.7*	10.8	13.3	13.3	*12.5*	11.8
Germany, Federal Republic of	6.9	6.0	4.3	3.7	2.7	*4.7*	4.1	5.5	5.9	*5.2*	5.4
Ireland	17.0	20.9	18.0	13.6	7.6	*15.3*	13.2	18.2	20.4	*17.2*	17.5
Italy	19.1	17.0	16.8	17.0	12.1	*16.4*	14.7	21.2	17.8	*17.9*	16.6
Netherlands	9.6	10.5	8.8	6.4	4.1	*7.9*	4.2	6.5	6.8	*5.8*	6.3
Weighted average EMS[3]	**11.5**	**10.3**	**8.6**	**7.9**	**6.2**	**8.9**	**7.6**	**10.2**	**10.0**	**9.3**	...
Arithmetic average EMS	**13.5**	**12.6**	**10.8**	**9.8**	**7.2**	**10.7**	**8.7**	**11.9**	**11.9**	**10.8**	**10.9**
Standard deviation	4.2	4.9	4.9	4.6	3.5	*4.2*	4.5	6.1	5.6	*5.4*	4.7
Difference between highest and lowest rate	12.1	14.9	13.7	13.3	9.4	...	10.6	15.7	14.5	...	12.1
Coefficient of variation	0.31	0.39	0.45	0.47	0.49	*0.42*	0.51	0.51	0.47	*0.50*	0.43
Average absolute deviation	3.1	3.6	3.8	3.6	2.9	*3.4*	3.8	4.9	4.9	*4.6*	3.7
Japan	24.4	11.8	9.3	8.0	3.8	*11.3*	3.6	8.0	4.9	*5.5*	2.9
Sweden	9.9	9.8	10.3	11.4	9.9	*10.3*	7.3	13.7	12.1	*11.0*	8.8
Switzerland	9.7	6.7	1.7	1.6	0.8	*4.0*	3.6	4.1	6.5	*4.7*	5.7
United Kingdom	16.0	24.2	16.5	15.9	8.3	*16.1*	13.4	18.0	11.9	*14.4*	8.7
United States	11.0	9.1	5.8	6.5	7.6	*8.0*	11.3	13.5	10.4	*11.7*	6.2
Arithmetic average EMS	**14.2**	**12.3**	**8.7**	**8.7**	**6.1**	**10.0**	**7.8**	**11.5**	**9.2**	**9.5**	**6.5**
Standard deviation	6.3	6.9	5.5	5.4	3.7	*5.6*	4.4	5.4	3.3	*4.4*	2.4
Coefficient of variation	0.44	0.56	0.63	0.62	0.61	*0.57*	0.57	0.47	0.36	*0.47*	0.38
Average absolute deviation	4.8	4.7	4.0	4.0	3.0	*4.1*	3.6	4.3	2.8	*3.6*	1.8

Sources: International Monetary Fund, *International Financial Statistics*; and Fund staff estimates.
[1] Compound average growth rates.
[2] Fund staff estimates.
[3] Weighted by real GDP (using 1980 weights in 1981).

Statistical Tables

Table 13. GDP Deflators, 1974–81

(Annual change in percent)

	1974	1975	1976	1977	1978	Average[1] 1974–78	1979	1980	1981	Average[1] 1979–81
Belgium	12.2	12.7	7.7	7.4	4.2	*8.8*	4.0	4.4	5.0	*4.5*
Denmark	13.0	12.4	8.7	8.8	9.7	*10.5*	6.5	9.0	9.5	*8.3*
France	11.1	13.4	9.9	9.0	9.5	*10.6*	10.3	11.8	12.0	*11.4*
Germany, Federal Republic of	6.8	6.7	3.2	3.8	3.8	*4.8*	3.7	4.9	4.3	*4.3*
Ireland	6.4	22.2	20.1	12.2	10.6	*14.3*	12.6	14.2	17.3	*14.7*
Italy	18.5	17.5	18.0	19.5	13.9	*17.5*	15.9	20.8	17.6	*18.1*
Netherlands	9.2	11.2	8.9	6.3	5.2	*8.1*	4.1	5.0	5.5	*4.9*
Weighted average EMS[2]	**10.4**	**11.2**	**8.3**	**8.0**	**7.1**	**9.0**	**7.3**	**9.0**	**8.6**	**8.3**
Arithmetic average EMS	**11.0**	**13.7**	**10.9**	**9.6**	**8.1**	**10.6**	**8.2**	**10.0**	**10.2**	**9.5**
Standard deviation	4.1	4.9	6.0	5.1	3.8	*4.8*	4.8	6.1	5.7	*5.5*
Difference between highest and lowest rate	12.0	15.5	16.9	15.7	10.1	...	12.1	16.4	13.3	...
Coefficient of variation	0.37	0.36	0.55	0.53	0.47	*0.46*	0.59	0.61	0.56	*0.59*
Average absolute deviation	3.3	3.5	4.6	3.6	3.2	*3.6*	4.1	4.8	4.7	*4.5*
Japan	20.6	8.1	6.4	5.7	4.6	*8.9*	2.6	3.0	2.9	*2.8*
Sweden	8.4	14.9	11.4	10.8	10.0	*11.1*	7.4	11.8	9.9	*9.7*
Switzerland[3]	7.1	6.9	3.1	0.3	3.4	*4.1*	2.1	3.1	6.7	*4.0*
United Kingdom	14.9	26.9	14.6	14.0	10.9	*16.1*	15.0	18.8	12.5	*15.4*
United States	8.9	9.3	5.2	5.8	7.4	*7.3*	8.6	9.3	9.4	*9.1*
Arithmetic average non-EMS	**12.0**	**13.2**	**8.1**	**7.3**	**7.3**	**9.6**	**7.1**	**9.2**	**8.3**	**8.2**
Standard deviation	5.7	8.2	4.7	5.3	3.3	*5.4*	5.2	6.6	3.6	*5.1*
Coefficient of variation	0.47	0.6	0.58	0.72	0.45	*0.57*	0.73	0.72	0.44	*0.63*
Average absolute deviation	4.6	6.1	3.9	4.1	2.6	*4.3*	3.8	4.9	4.4	*3.0*

Sources: International Monetary Fund, *World Economic Outlook* (various issues); and Fund staff calculations.
[1] Compound average growth rates.
[2] Weighted by real GDP (using 1980 weights in 1981).
[3] GNP deflator.

Table 14. Short-Term Interest Rates, 1974–81

(Monthly averages in percent)

	1974	1975	1976	1977	1978	Average 1974–78	1979	1980	1981	Average 1979–81
Belgium	9.3	4.7	8.3	5.5	5.2	*6.6*	8.0	11.2	11.5	*10.2*
Denmark	13.3	6.5	10.3	14.5	15.4	*12.0*	12.6	16.9	14.8	*14.8*
France	12.9	7.9	8.6	9.1	8.0	*9.3*	9.0	11.9	15.3	*12.1*
Germany, Federal Republic of	9.9	5.0	4.3	4.4	3.7	*5.5*	6.7	9.5	12.1	*9.4*
Ireland	11.3	10.0	10.8	7.7	8.4	*9.6*	13.5	15.4	13.5	*14.1*
Italy	14.6	10.6	15.7	14.0	11.5	*13.3*	11.9	17.2	19.6	*16.2*
Netherlands	9.2	4.2	7.3	3.8	6.2	*6.1*	9.0	10.1	11.0	*10.0*
Weighted average EMS[1]	**11.3**	**6.5**	**7.8**	**7.3**	**6.8**	**7.9**	**8.6**	**11.7**	**13.6**	**11.3**
Arithmetic average EMS	**11.4**	**6.9**	**9.3**	**8.4**	**8.4**	**8.9**	**10.0**	**13.1**	**13.9**	**12.4**
Standard deviation	2.3	2.7	3.5	4.4	4.0	*3.3*	2.8	3.3	3.1	*2.9*
Difference between highest and lowest rate	5.4	6.4	11.4	10.7	11.7	...	6.8	7.7	8.6	...
Coefficient of variation	0.20	0.39	0.38	0.52	0.48	*0.39*	0.28	0.25	0.22	*0.24*
Average absolute deviation	1.8	2.2	2.5	3.5	2.9	*2.6*	2.2	2.9	2.2	*2.4*
Japan	12.5	10.7	7.0	5.7	4.4	*8.1*	5.9	10.9	7.4	*8.1*
Sweden	7.5	7.8	7.9	10.0	7.2	*8.1*	8.2	12.2	14.4	*11.6*
United Kingdom	11.4	10.6	11.6	8.1	3.7	*9.1*	13.6	16.1	13.3	*14.3*
United States	10.5	5.8	5.1	5.5	7.9	*7.0*	11.2	13.4	16.4	*13.7*
Arithmetic average non-EMS	**10.5**	**8.7**	**7.9**	**7.3**	**5.8**	**8.0**	**9.7**	**13.2**	**12.9**	**11.9**
Standard deviation	2.2	2.4	2.7	2.1	2.1	*2.3*	3.4	2.2	3.9	*3.2*
Coefficient of variation	0.21	0.27	0.35	0.29	0.36	*0.29*	0.35	0.17	0.30	*0.27*
Average absolute deviation	1.5	1.9	1.9	1.7	1.8	*1.8*	2.7	1.6	2.7	*2.3*

Source: International Monetary Fund, *International Financial Statistics*.
[1] Weighted by real GDP (using 1980 weights in 1981).

APPENDIX I • STATISTICAL TABLES

Table 15. Long-Term Interest Rates, 1974–81
(Monthly averages in percent)

	1974	1975	1976	1977	1978	Average 1974–78	1979	1980	1981	Average 1979–81
Belgium	8.7	8.5	9.1	8.8	8.5	*8.7*	9.5	12.0	13.7	*11.7*
Denmark	14.6	13.1	13.2	13.4	14.5	*13.8*	15.8	17.7	18.9	*17.5*
France	10.5	9.5	9.2	9.6	9.0	*9.6*	9.5	13.0	15.7	*12.7*
Germany, Federal Republic of	10.4	8.5	7.8	6.2	5.8	*7.7*	7.4	8.5	10.4	*8.8*
Ireland	16.9	14.6	15.5	11.3	12.8	*14.2*	15.1	15.4	17.3	*15.9*
Italy	9.9	11.5	13.1	14.6	13.7	*12.6*	14.1	16.1	20.6	*16.9*
Netherlands	9.8	8.8	9.0	8.1	7.7	*8.7*	8.8	10.2	11.6	*10.2*
Weighted average EMS[1]	**10.4**	**9.4**	**9.4**	**8.9**	**8.5**	**9.3**	**9.5**	**11.6**	**13.7**	**11.6**
Arithmetic average EMS	**11.5**	**10.7**	**11.0**	**10.3**	**10.3**	**10.7**	**11.4**	**13.3**	**15.4**	**13.4**
Standard deviation	3.0	2.5	2.9	3.0	3.4	*3.0*	3.4	3.3	3.8	*3.5*
Difference between highest and lowest rate	8.2	6.1	7.7	8.4	8.7	...	8.4	9.2	10.2	...
Coefficient of variation	0.26	0.23	0.27	0.29	0.33	*0.28*	0.30	0.25	0.24	*0.26*
Average absolute deviation	2.4	2.1	2.5	2.4	2.7	*2.4*	3.0	2.7	3.1	*2.9*
Japan	9.3	9.2	8.7	7.3	6.1	*8.1*	7.7	9.2	8.7	*8.5*
Sweden	7.8	8.8	9.3	9.7	10.1	*9.1*	10.5	11.7	13.5	*11.9*
Switzerland	7.2	6.4	5.0	4.1	3.3	*5.2*	3.5	4.8	5.6	*4.6*
United Kingdom	14.8	14.4	14.4	12.7	12.5	*13.8*	13.0	13.8	14.7	*13.8*
United States	8.1	8.2	7.9	7.7	8.5	*8.1*	9.3	11.4	13.7	*11.5*
Arithmetic average non-EMS	**9.4**	**9.4**	**9.1**	**8.3**	**8.1**	**8.9**	**8.8**	**10.2**	**11.2**	**10.1**
Standard deviation	3.1	3.0	3.4	3.2	3.6	3.3	3.5	3.4	3.9	*3.6*
Coefficient of variation	0.33	0.32	0.38	0.38	0.44	*0.37*	0.40	0.34	0.35	*0.36*
Average absolute deviation	2.1	2.0	1.9	2.3	2.7	*2.2*	3.3	2.5	3.3	*3.0*

Source: International Monetary Fund, *International Financial Statistics*.
[1] Weighted by real GDP (using 1980 weights in 1981).

Table 16. Matrix of Correlation Coefficients Between Long-Term Interest Rates, March 1976–March 1979 and April 1979–March 1982[1]

(Monthly averages)

	Denmark	France	Fed. Rep. of Germany	Ireland	Italy	Netherlands	United Kingdom	United States
Belgium	−0.445	0.239	0.768	0.767	−0.012	0.642	0.681	−0.422
	0.792	0.979	0.882	0.663	0.906	0.913	0.771	0.933
Denmark		−0.517	−0.272	−0.445	−0.210	−0.258	−0.357	0.573
		0.811	0.640	0.602	0.834	0.732	0.652	0.793
France			−0.079	0.213	0.628	0.050	−0.015	−0.843
			0.904	0.718	0.944	0.923	0.795	0.941
Germany, Federal Republic of				0.822	−0.461	0.893	0.783	−0.221
				0.718	0.899	0.947	0.742	0.906
Ireland					−0.188	0.667	0.923	−0.456
					0.741	0.651	0.777	0.753
Italy						−0.314	−0.272	−0.452
						0.883	0.722	0.822
Netherlands							0.645	−0.204
							0.788	0.836
United Kingdom								−0.239
								0.792

Sources: International Monetary Fund, *International Financial Statistics*; and Fund staff estimates.
[1] Line 1 shows the correlation coefficient for the period March 1976 to March 1979 and line 2, the correlation coefficient for the period April 1979 to March 1982.

Table 17. Matrix of Correlation Coefficients Between Short-Term Interest Rates, March 1976–March 1979 and April 1979–March 1982[1]

(Monthly averages)

	Denmark	France	Fed. Rep. of Germany	Ireland	Italy	Netherlands	United Kingdom	United States
Belgium	0.102	0.310	0.480	0.532	0.537	0.627	0.601	−0.290
	0.445	0.502	0.629	0.488	0.565	0.463	0.340	0.335
Denmark		0.201	−0.142	−0.186	−0.371	0.032	−0.334	0.100
		0.398	0.340	0.605	0.175	0.456	0.510	0.120
France			0.505	0.055	0.433	0.050	0.321	−0.730
			0.809	0.560	0.783	0.644	−0.032	0.550
Germany, Federal Republic of				0.560	0.605	0.312	0.763	−0.454
				0.050	0.809	0.567	−0.151	0.654
Ireland					0.388	0.524	0.716	0.043
					−0.024	0.415	0.800	−0.052
Italy						0.115	0.713	−0.775
						0.436	−0.021	0.547
Netherlands							0.323	0.210
							0.404	0.262
United Kingdom								−0.392
								−0.221

Sources: International Monetary Fund, *International Financial Statistics*; and Fund staff estimates.

[1] For every country, line 1 indicates the correlation coefficient for the three-year period (March 1976–March 1979) prior to the introduction of the EMS and line 2 indicates the correlation coefficient for the three-year period from April 1979 to March 1982.

Table 18. Rate of Growth of Narrow Money, 1974–81

(Annual change in percent)

	1974	1975	1976	1977	1978	Average[1] 1974-78	1979	1980	1981	Average[1] 1979-81
Belgium	6.2	15.7	7.0	8.3	5.9	*8.6*	2.5	0.2	2.2	*1.6*
Denmark	4.7	30.2	6.3	8.0	16.1	*12.7*	9.9	10.9	11.8	*10.9*
France	15.2	12.6	7.5	11.1	11.1	*11.5*	11.8	6.4	15.9	*11.4*
Germany, Federal Republic of	10.7	14.3	3.3	12.0	14.5	*10.9*	2.9	3.9	−1.6	*1.7*
Ireland	9.0	19.9	16.9	22.5	27.6	*19.2*	8.1	14.0	3.4	*8.5*
Italy	9.4	13.5	18.9	21.4	26.6	*18.0*	23.7	12.9	9.8	*15.5*
Netherlands	12.2	19.7	8.2	13.2	4.2	*11.5*	2.8	6.0	−2.4	*2.1*
Arithmetic average EMS	**9.6**	**18.0**	**9.7**	**13.8**	**15.1**	**13.2**	**8.8**	**7.8**	**5.6**	**7.4**
Standard deviation	3.5	6.1	5.8	5.9	9.2	*6.1*	7.6	5.0	7.0	*6.5*
Coefficient of variation	0.37	0.34	0.60	0.43	0.61	*0.47*	0.86	0.65	1.25	*0.92*
Average absolute deviation	2.6	4.5	4.7	4.7	7.0	*3.0*	5.4	4.2	5.9	*5.2*
Japan	11.5	11.1	12.5	8.2	13.4	*11.3*	3.0	−2.0	10.0	*3.6*
Sweden	13.8	14.1	3.6	10.1	17.1	*11.6*	15.6	18.3	8.0	*13.9*
Switzerland	−1.4	4.9	11.2	7.5	22.9	*8.7*	−2.8	−0.9	2.7	*−0.4*
United Kingdom	10.8	...	11.3	21.5	16.4	...	9.1	3.9	...	...
United States	3.1	5.5	5.9	8.2	8.1	*6.1*	8.0	5.5	5.5	*6.3*
Arithmetic average non-EMS	**7.6**	...	**8.9**	**11.1**	**15.4**	...	**6.6**	**5.0**	...	...
Standard deviation	6.4	...	3.9	5.9	5.4	...	6.9	8.1	...	...
Coefficient of variation	0.85	...	0.44	0.53	0.35	...	1.0	1.6	...	...
Average absolute deviation	5.4	...	3.3	4.2	3.9	...	5.2	5.6	...	...

Source: International Monetary Fund, *International Financial Statistics*.

[1] Compound average growth rates.

APPENDIX I • STATISTICAL TABLES

Table 19. Rate of Growth of Broad Money, 1974-81[1,2]

(Annual change in percent)

	1974	1975	1976	1977	1978	Average[3] 1974-78	1979	1980	1981	Average[3] 1979-81
Belgium	8.7	15.3	12.6	8.4	7.5	*10.5*	6.2	3.3	6.5	*5.3*
Denmark	8.4	26.9	11.7	9.3	6.4	*12.3*	10.2	11.7	10.8	*10.9*
France	17.8	15.7	12.3	14.6	12.2	*14.5*	13.9	8.3	11.1	*11.1*
Germany, Federal Republic of	7.2	11.5	7.6	10.3	10.3	*9.4*	5.2	4.6	3.7	*4.5*
Ireland	19.3	21.7	13.0	20.6	23.5	*19.6*	13.6	20.6	10.8	*14.9*
Italy	15.7	24.4	21.0	22.2	23.0	*21.2*	19.4	12.2	10.2	*13.9*
Netherlands	16.1	12.9	17.1	12.9	11.4	*14.0*	11.6	5.6	7.8	*8.3*
Weighted average EMS[4]	**12.8**	**16.6**	**13.3**	**14.5**	**13.8**	**14.2**	**11.5**	**7.7**	**7.9**	**9.0**
Arithmetic average EMS	**13.3**	**18.4**	**13.6**	**14.0**	**13.5**	**14.5**	**11.4**	**9.5**	**8.7**	**9.8**
Standard deviation	5.0	6.0	4.3	5.5	7.0	*5.6*	4.9	6.0	2.8	*4.6*
Coefficient of variation	0.38	0.33	0.31	0.39	0.52	*0.39*	0.43	0.63	0.33	*0.46*
Average absolute deviation	4.5	5.1	3.1	4.4	5.6	*4.5*	3.6	4.6	2.3	*3.3*
Japan	11.5	14.5	13.5	11.1	13.1	*12.7*	8.4	6.8	10.7	*8.6*
Sweden	9.7	11.6	5.1	9.1	17.4	*10.5*	17.1	12.2	13.3	*14.2*
Switzerland	5.0	7.5	8.5	6.9	10.5	*7.7*	10.0	3.9	6.9	*6.9*
United Kingdom	12.9	...	11.6	9.8	14.6	...	12.5	18.4	...	...
United States	4.6	10.2	12.5	8.1	5.4	*8.1*	8.0	7.8	7.2	*7.6*
Arithmetic average non-EMS	**8.7**	...	**10.2**	**9.0**	**12.2**	...	**11.2**	**9.8**	...	...
Standard deviation	3.9	...	3.5	1.6	4.5	...	3.7	5.6	...	...
Coefficient of variation	0.45	...	0.34	0.18	0.37	...	0.32	0.57	...	...
Average absolute deviation	3.2	...	2.8	1.2	3.4	...	2.9	4.4	...	...

Source: International Monetary Fund, *International Financial Statistics*.
[1] Broad money (M2) defined as money and quasi-money.
[2] End-of-year data.
[3] Compound average growth rates.
[4] Weighted by the broad money stock in the previous year converted into dollars using the average dollar exchange rate.

Table 20. Rate of Growth of Domestic Credit, 1974-81

(Annual change in percent)

	1974	1975	1976	1977	1978	Average[1] 1974-78	1979	1980	1981	Average[1] 1979-81
Belgium	10.6	13.8	16.3	15.2	10.8	*13.3*	14.8	11.5	12.9	*13.1*
Denmark	10.4	26.7	14.7	3.4	4.2	*11.6*	12.3	13.3	14.5	*13.4*
France	19.3	17.1	21.1	20.7	8.8	*17.3*	14.0	12.3	14.0	*13.4*
Germany, Federal Republic of	8.0	10.1	10.6	10.0	11.4	*10.0*	11.9	9.5	8.8	*10.1*
Ireland	19.5	18.1	12.9	20.4	30.1	*20.1*	30.4	15.3	15.2	*20.1*
Italy	23.8	23.5	21.4	16.3	17.4	*20.4*	16.0	16.6	12.6	*15.1*
Netherlands	16.5	14.3	19.7	23.1	21.0	*18.9*	17.2	10.4	5.9	*11.1*
Average EMS	**15.4**	**17.7**	**16.7**	**15.6**	**14.8**	**15.9**	**16.7**	**12.7**	**12.0**	**13.8**
Standard deviation	5.9	5.8	4.2	6.9	8.7	*6.3*	6.3	2.6	3.4	*4.1*
Coefficient of variation	0.38	0.33	0.25	0.44	0.59	*0.40*	0.38	0.20	0.28	*0.29*
Average absolute deviation	5.0	4.4	3.5	5.2	6.9	*5.0*	4.1	2.0	2.6	*2.9*
Japan	15.0	16.7	13.7	10.5	13.7	*13.9*	8.4	8.4	10.0	*8.9*
Sweden	12.8	13.6	7.8	11.5	19.5	*13.0*	18.2	13.4	18.6	*16.7*
Switzerland	5.9	6.2	7.1	6.6	8.6	*6.9*	8.9	11.1	8.5	*9.5*
United Kingdom	17.5	...	13.8	6.0	10.0	...	9.8	14.3	...	...
United States	9.9	4.4	8.1	10.3	11.0	*8.7*	11.4	7.7	8.7	*9.3*
Average non-EMS	**12.2**	...	**10.1**	**9.0**	**12.6**	...	**11.4**	**11.0**	...	...
Standard deviation	4.6	...	3.4	2.4	4.3	...	4.0	2.8	...	...
Coefficient of variation	0.37	...	0.33	0.27	0.34	...	0.35	0.26	...	...
Average absolute deviation	3.5	...	2.9	2.1	3.2	...	2.8	2.3	...	...

Source: International Monetary Fund, *International Financial Statistics*.
[1] Compound average growth rates.

Statistical Tables

Table 21. Real Narrow Money Stock, 1974-81[1]
(Annual change in percent)

	1974	1975	1976	1977	1978	Average 1974-78	1979	1980	1981	Average 1979-81
Belgium	−5.8	2.7	−2.0	1.1	1.0	−0.6	−1.8	−6.0	−5.1	−4.3
Denmark	−9.1	18.8	−2.5	−2.8	5.5	2.0	0.3	−1.2	0.1	−0.3
France	1.3	0.7	−1.9	1.6	1.8	0.7	0.9	−6.1	2.3	−1.0
Germany, Federal Republic of	3.6	7.8	−1.0	8.0	11.5	6.0	−1.2	−1.5	−7.1	−3.2
Ireland	−6.8	−0.8	−0.9	7.8	18.6	3.6	−4.5	−3.6	−14.1	−7.5
Italy	−8.1	−3.0	1.8	3.8	12.9	1.5	7.8	−6.8	−6.8	−2.2
Netherlands	2.4	8.3	−0.6	6.4	0.1	3.3	−1.3	−0.5	−8.5	−3.5
Arithmetic average EMS	**−3.3**	**4.9**	**−1.0**	**3.7**	**7.3**	*2.2*	—	**−3.7**	**−5.6**	*−3.1*
Standard deviation	5.4	7.4	1.4	4.0	7.0	*2.1*	3.8	2.6	5.5	*4.0*
Coefficient of variation	−1.7	1.5	−1.4	1.1	1.0	*1.0*	...	−0.72	−1.0	...
Average absolute deviation	4.8	5.8	1.0	3.2	5.9	*1.7*	2.4	2.3	4.0	*1.7*

Source: Tables 12 and 18.
[1] Deflated by the consumer price index.

Table 22. Real Broad Money Stock, 1974-81[1]
(Annual change in percent)

	1974	1975	1976	1977	1978	Average 1974-78	1979	1980	1981	Average 1979-81
Belgium	−3.5	2.3	3.1	1.2	2.9	*1.1*	1.6	−3.1	−1.1	*−1.0*
Denmark	−5.9	15.8	2.5	−1.6	−3.3	*1.5*	0.5	−0.5	−0.8	*−0.3*
France	3.6	3.5	2.5	4.8	2.8	*3.5*	2.8	−4.4	−1.9	*−1.2*
Germany, Federal Republic of	0.3	5.2	3.2	6.4	7.4	*4.5*	1.1	−0.9	−2.1	*−0.7*
Ireland	2.0	0.7	−4.2	6.2	14.8	*3.9*	0.4	2.0	−8.0	*−1.9*
Italy	−2.9	6.3	3.6	4.4	9.7	*4.3*	4.1	−7.4	−6.5	*−3.3*
Netherlands	5.9	2.2	7.6	6.1	7.0	*5.8*	7.1	−0.8	0.9	*2.4*
Arithmetic average EMS	**−0.1**	**5.1**	**2.5**	**3.9**	**5.9**	*3.4*	2.5	**−2.2**	**−2.8**	*−0.8*
Standard deviation	4.2	5.1	3.5	3.0	5.8	*1.7*	2.4	3.1	3.3	*1.7*
Coefficient of variation	−42.0	1.0	1.4	0.8	1.0	*0.5*	1.0	−1.4	−1.2	*−2.1*
Average absolute deviation	3.5	3.4	2.0	2.4	4.4	*1.3*	1.8	2.4	2.6	*1.1*

Source: Tables 12 and 19.
[1] Deflated by the consumer price index.

Table 23. Real Domestic Credit, 1974-81[1]
(Annual change in percent)

	1974	1975	1976	1977	1978	Average[2] 1974-78	1979	1980	1981	Average[2] 1979-81
Belgium	−1.9	1.0	6.5	7.6	6.0	*3.8*	9.9	4.6	4.9	*6.4*
Denmark	−4.2	15.6	5.2	−6.9	−5.3	*0.5*	2.5	0.9	2.5	*2.0*
France	4.9	4.7	10.5	10.3	−0.3	*5.9*	2.9	−0.9	0.6	*0.9*
Germany, Federal Republic of	1.0	3.9	6.0	6.1	8.5	*5.1*	7.5	3.8	2.7	*4.6*
Ireland	2.1	−2.3	−4.3	6.0	20.9	*4.1*	15.2	−2.5	−4.3	*2.4*
Italy	3.9	5.6	3.9	−0.6	4.7	*3.5*	1.1	−3.8	−4.4	*−2.4*
Netherlands	6.3	3.4	10.0	15.7	16.2	*10.2*	12.5	3.7	−0.8	*5.0*
Arithmetic average EMS	**1.7**	**4.6**	**5.4**	**5.5**	**7.2**	*4.7*	**7.4**	**0.8**	**0.2**	*2.7*
Standard deviation	3.8	5.5	4.9	7.3	9.0	*2.9*	5.4	3.3	3.6	*3.0*
Coefficient of variation	2.2	1.2	0.9	1.3	1.3	*0.6*	0.7	4.1	18.1	*1.1*
Average absolute deviation	2.9	3.5	3.3	5.2	6.7	*2.0*	4.5	2.8	2.9	*2.3*

Source: Tables 12 and 20.
[1] Deflated by the consumer price index.
[2] Compound average growth rates.

APPENDIX I • STATISTICAL TABLES

Table 24. Central Government Budget Deficit as a Ratio to Nominal GDP, 1974–81
(In percent)

	1974	1975	1976	1977	1978	Average 1974–78	1979	1980	1981	Average 1979–81
Belgium	2.8	4.7	5.1	5.9	6.0	*4.9*	6.5	8.7	12.2	*9.1*
Denmark	−3.0	3.5	2.8	2.6	2.8	*1.7*	3.7	4.8	8.3	*5.6*
France	−0.3	3.0	0.8	0.8	0.8	*1.0*	0.1	—	1.1	*0.4*
Germany, Federal Republic of	1.0	3.3	2.7	1.9	2.0	*2.2*	1.9	1.9	2.5	*2.1*
Ireland	11.8	13.4	10.8	10.1	13.3	*11.9*	14.1	14.7	17.2	*15.3*
Italy	8.1	13.1	9.3	11.8	15.4	*11.5*	11.1	11.0	13.4	*11.8*
Netherlands	0.6	3.1	3.6	2.9	3.1	*2.7*	4.2	4.6	6.0	*4.9*
Weighted average EMS[1]	1.6	4.7	3.4	3.4	3.9	*3.4*	3.4	3.6	5.0	*4.0*
Arithmetic average EMS	3.0	6.3	5.0	5.1	6.2	*5.1*	5.9	6.5	8.7	*7.0*
Standard deviation	5.2	4.8	3.7	4.3	5.8	*4.8*	5.1	5.2	5.9	*5.4*
Coefficient of variation	1.72	0.76	0.74	0.84	0.94	*1.0*	0.85	0.80	0.68	*0.78*
Average absolute deviation	4.0	4.0	2.9	3.5	4.7	*3.8*	4.0	4.2	4.8	*4.3*
Japan	1.3	4.8	2.0	6.2	6.6	*4.2*	5.4	6.2	5.3	*5.6*
Switzerland	0.6	1.3	1.0	0.9	—	*0.8*	1.5	—	0.8	*0.8*
United Kingdom	4.2	8.0	5.4	3.1	5.1	*5.2*	5.4	5.0	4.1	*4.8*
United States	0.8	4.9	3.3	2.7	2.1	*2.8*	1.2	2.7	2.5	*2.1*
Arithmetic average non-EMS	1.7	4.8	2.9	3.2	3.5	*3.3*	3.4	3.5	3.2	*3.4*
Standard deviation	1.7	2.7	1.9	2.2	3.0	*2.3*	2.3	2.7	2.0	*2.3*
Coefficient of variation	0.97	0.58	0.65	0.68	0.86	*0.75*	0.69	0.79	0.62	*0.7*
Average absolute deviation	1.2	1.7	1.1	1.2	2.4	*1.5*	2.0	1.3	1.5	*1.6*

Sources: International Monetary Fund, *International Financial Statistics*; and national authorities.
[1] Weighted by real GDP in the current year (using 1980 weights in 1981).

Table 25. Budget Deficits and Changes in Money Supply, 1974–81[1]
(In percent)

	1974	1975	1976	1977	1978	Average 1974–78	1979	1980	1981	Average 1979–81
Belgium	31.0	41.2	60.5	81.2	86.7	*60.1*	170.7	515.9	297.8	*328.1*
Denmark	−48.8	19.9	16.1	40.3	78.7	*21.2*	77.5	130.4	163.8	*123.9*
Germany, Federal Republic of	38.2	154.6	97.6	49.2	54.5	*78.8*	106.8	118.9	189.1	*138.3*
France	−8.8	27.1	8.1	12.4	31.2	*14.0*	12.4	−9.9	36.7	*13.1*
Ireland	59.9	105.6	97.0	79.8	56.2	*79.7*	108.0	124.1	144.9	*125.7*
Italy	56.1	60.2	48.3	40.4	46.0	*50.2*	46.1	56.3	84.3	*62.2*
Netherlands	1.5	144.5	34.5	116.7	160.1	*91.5*	139.3	248.7	288.0	*225.3*

Source: *European Economy*, No. 12 (July 1982), p. 28.
[1] General government borrowing requirement (+) or financial surplus (−) divided by the increase in broad money supply.

Table 26. Balance of Payments Current Account, 1974–81
(In billions of U.S. dollars)

	1974	1975	1976	1977	1978	Average 1974–78	1979	1980	1981	Average 1979–81
Belgium	0.6	0.3	—	−0.7	−1.0	*−0.2*	−3.0	−5.2	...	...
Denmark	−1.0	−0.5	−1.9	−1.7	−1.5	*−1.3*	−3.0	−2.5	−1.9	*−2.4*
France	−5.8	−0.2	−5.7	−3.1	3.3	*−2.3*	1.2	−7.9	−7.3	*−4.6*
Germany, Federal Republic of	10.4	4.1	3.9	4.1	9.2	*6.3*	−6.1	−16.5	−7.2	*−9.9*
Ireland	−0.7	−0.1	−0.3	−0.4	−0.5	*−0.4*	−1.7	−1.7	...	...
Italy	−8.1	−0.6	−2.9	2.4	6.2	*−0.6*	5.4	−9.8	−8.7	*−4.4*
Netherlands	2.2	2.0	2.7	0.6	−1.4	*1.2*	−2.1	−2.8	3.2	*−0.6*
Arithmetic average EMS	−0.3	0.7	−0.6	0.2	2.0	*0.4*	−1.3	−6.6	...	...
Japan	−4.7	−0.7	3.7	10.9	17.5	*5.4*	−8.8	−10.8	4.8	*−4.9*
Sweden	−0.6	−0.3	−1.6	−2.2	−0.3	*−1.0*	−2.4	−4.4	−2.8	*−3.2*
Switzerland	0.2	2.6	3.5	3.8	4.4	*2.9*	2.4	−0.6	2.6	*1.5*
United Kingdom	−7.7	−3.5	−1.6	—	2.0	*−2.1*	−1.7	6.9	12.7	*6.0*
United States	2.1	18.3	4.4	−14.1	−14.8	*−0.8*	−0.5	1.5	4.4	*1.8*

Source: International Monetary Fund, *International Financial Statistics*.

36

Statistical Tables

Table 27. The Creation of ECUs by Swap Operations, April 1979-December 1982

Swap Operations Starting In	Gold Transfers (million ounces)	U.S. Dollar Transfers (billions)	Gold Price (ECUs per ounce)	US $1 = ... ECU	Counterpart in ECUs (billions) Gold	Counterpart in ECUs (billions) U.S. dollars	Counterpart in ECUs (billions) Total
Apr. 1979	80.7	13.4	165	0.75	13.3	10.0	23.3
July 1979[1]	85.3	15.9	185	0.73	15.8	11.6	27.4
Oct. 1979	85.3	16.0	211	0.70	18.0	11.3	29.3
Jan. 1980	85.5	15.5	259	0.69	22.2	10.7	32.9
Apr. 1980	85.6	14.4	370	0.77	31.7	11.1	42.8
July 1980	85.6	13.7	419	0.70	35.9	9.6	45.5
Oct. 1980	85.6	13.9	425	0.71	36.4	9.9	46.3
Jan. 1981	85.6	14.5	447	0.75	38.3	10.9	49.2
Apr. 1981	85.7	14.2	440	0.84	37.7	12.0	49.7
July 1981	85.7	12.7	406	0.97	34.8	12.3	47.1
Oct. 1981	85.7	11.5	402	0.91	34.5	10.5	45.0
Jan. 1982	85.7	11.7	368	0.92	31.6	10.7	42.3
Apr. 1982	85.7	10.5	327	1.00	28.0	10.5	38.6
July 1982	85.7	9.9	324	1.04	27.8	10.3	38.1
Oct. 1982	85.7	10.0	367	0.92	31.5	10.8	42.3
Dec. 1982	85.7	9.6	367	0.92	31.5	10.4	41.9

Source: Commission of the European Communities.
[1] The Bank of England transferred 20 percent of its gold and U.S. dollar reserves from July 1979. The Bank of Greece has made no transfer.

Table 28. Real Rates of Growth of Gross Domestic Product, 1974–81

(Annual change in percent)

	1974	1975	1976	1977	1978	Average[1] 1974–78	1979	1980	1981	Average[1] 1979–81
Belgium	4.6	−1.8	5.6	0.6	3.0	*2.4*	2.3	2.2	−1.6	*1.0*
Denmark	−0.9	−0.6	7.9	1.9	1.9	*2.0*	3.1	0.6	−0.2	*1.2*
France	3.3	0.2	5.2	3.1	3.8	*3.1*	3.3	1.1	0.2	*1.5*
Germany, Federal Republic of	0.4	−1.7	5.3	2.8	3.5	*2.1*	4.0	1.8	−0.2	*1.9*
Ireland	4.2	1.5	1.6	6.3	6.2	*4.0*	2.5	1.3	1.0	*1.6*
Italy	4.1	−3.6	5.9	1.9	2.7	*2.2*	4.9	3.9	−0.2	*2.9*
Luxembourg	3.6	−6.1	1.6	0.8	4.6	*0.9*	4.2	0.6	−3.3	*0.5*
Netherlands	3.6	−1.9	5.6	7.7	2.4	*3.5*	1.8	0.7	−1.0	*0.5*
Weighted average EMS[2]	**2.3**	**−1.4**	**5.5**	**3.1**	**3.3**	*2.6*	**3.7**	**1.7**	**−0.3**	*1.7*
Arithmetic average EMS	**2.9**	**−1.8**	**4.8**	**3.1**	**3.5**	*2.5*	**3.3**	**1.5**	**−0.7**	*1.4*
Standard deviation	2.0	2.3	2.2	2.5	1.4	*2.1*	1.1	1.1	1.4	*1.2*
Coefficient of variation	0.70	−1.31	0.45	0.81	0.39	*0.21*	0.33	0.74	−1.85	*−0.26*
Average absolute deviation	1.8	1.8	1.9	2.2	1.2	*1.8*	1.0	0.9	1.1	*1.0*
Japan	−1.2	2.4	5.3	5.3	5.1	*3.4*	5.2	4.2	2.9	*4.1*
Sweden	4.3	2.2	1.2	−2.0	1.3	*1.4*	4.3	1.8	−0.8	*1.8*
Switzerland[3]	1.7	−7.7	−0.4	2.8	0.4	*−0.6*	2.8	3.9	1.4	*2.7*
United Kingdom	−1.8	−1.0	2.8	2.2	3.7	*1.2*	1.9	−2.1	−2.2	*−0.8*
United States	−0.7	−1.2	5.4	5.5	5.0	*2.8*	2.8	−0.4	1.9	*1.4*
Arithmetic average non-EMS	**0.5**	**−1.1**	**2.9**	**2.8**	**3.1**	*1.6*	**3.4**	**1.5**	**0.6**	*1.8*
Standard deviation	2.5	4.1	2.5	3.0	2.2	*2.9*	1.3	2.7	2.1	*2.0*
Coefficient of variation	5.49	−3.85	0.89	0.10	0.69	*0.86*	0.39	1.84	3.26	*1.83*
Average absolute deviation	2.0	2.7	2.0	1.3	1.8	*2.0*	1.1	0.5	1.7	*1.1*

Sources: International Monetary Fund, *World Economic Outlook* (various issues) and Fund staff calculations.
[1] Compound average growth rate.
[2] Weighted by the real GDP in the previous year, converted into U.S. dollars using the dollar exchange rate of 1975.
[3] Rate of growth of real GNP.

APPENDIX I • STATISTICAL TABLES

Table 29. Gross Fixed Capital Formation, 1974–81
(In percent of GDP)

	1974	1975	1976	1977	1978	Average 1974–78	1979	1980	1981	Average 1979–81
Belgium	22.3	22.1	21.6	21.3	21.1	*21.7*	20.2	21.0	...	...
Denmark	24.0	21.1	23.0	22.1	21.7	*22.4*	21.0	18.4	15.6	*18.3*
France	24.3	23.3	23.3	22.3	21.4	*22.9*	21.4	21.6	21.0	*21.3*
Germany, Federal Republic of	21.9	20.7	20.7	20.7	20.7	*20.9*	21.8	22.8	22.0	*22.2*
Ireland	25.2	23.3	24.7	25.0	27.8	*25.2*	31.3	29.4	29.7	*30.1*
Italy	22.4	20.6	20.0	19.6	18.7	*20.3*	18.8	19.8	20.3	*19.6*
Netherlands	21.8	20.8	19.2	21.1	21.3	*20.8*	21.1	21.0	19.0	*20.4*
Arithmetic average EMS	**23.1**	**21.7**	**21.8**	**21.7**	**21.8**	**22.0**	**22.2**	**22.0**	...	...
Weighted average EMS[1]	**22.7**	**21.5**	**21.3**	**21.1**	**21.0**	**21.5**	**21.4**	**21.8**	...	...
Standard deviation	1.3	1.2	2.0	1.7	2.8	*1.8*	4.1	3.6	...	...
Difference between highest and lowest rate	3.4	2.7	5.5	5.4	9.1	...	12.5	11.0	...	...
Coefficient of variation	0.06	0.06	0.09	0.08	0.13	*0.08*	0.18	0.16	...	...
Average absolute deviation	1.1	1.0	1.6	1.2	1.7	*1.3*	2.6	2.5	...	...
Japan	34.8	32.4	31.3	30.5	30.8	*32.0*	32.1	32.0	...	...
Sweden	21.5	21.0	21.1	21.2	19.4	*20.8*	19.9	20.1	19.2	*19.7*
Switzerland	27.6	24.0	20.6	20.7	21.4	*22.9*	21.8	23.8	24.6	*23.4*
United Kingdom	20.3	19.5	18.9	17.9	18.0	*18.9*	17.9	17.7	...	...
United States	15.2	13.9	14.5	15.9	16.9	*15.3*	17.2	15.9	15.6	*16.2*
Arithmetic average non-EMS	**23.9**	**22.2**	**21.3**	**21.2**	**21.3**	**22.0**	**21.8**	**21.9**	...	...
Standard deviation	7.5	6.8	6.2	5.6	5.6	*6.3*	6.0	6.4	...	...
Coefficient of variation	0.32	0.31	0.29	0.26	0.26	*0.29*	0.28	0.29	...	...
Average absolute deviation	5.9	4.8	4.0	3.7	3.8	*4.4*	4.1	4.8	...	...

Source: International Monetary Fund, *International Financial Statistics*.
[1] Weighted by real GDP (using 1980 weights in 1981).

Appendix II
Bibliography

International Monetary Fund

Annual Report of the Executive Board (various issues).
Annual Report on Exchange Arrangements and Exchange Restrictions (various issues).
IMF Survey, Vol. 7 (December 13, 1978), pp. 369, 376–77, 378–79; Vol. 8 (March 19, 1979), pp. 81, 93; and Supplement: The European Monetary System, pp. 97–100; (June 18, 1979), p. 186; Vol. 10 (April 6, 1981), p. 111; (December 14, 1981), p. 385; Vol. 11 (March 8, 1982), p. 76; (June 21, 1982), pp. 188–89; (July 5, 1982), p. 206; Vol. 12 (April 4, 1983), pp. 97, 103.
World Economic Outlook: A Survey by the Staff of the International Monetary Fund (Washington, May 1980).
World Economic Outlook: A Survey by the Staff of the International Monetary Fund, Occasional Paper No. 4 (Washington, June 1981).
World Economic Outlook: A Survey by the Staff of the International Monetary Fund, Occasional Paper No. 9 (Washington, April 1982).

European Communities

Treaties Establishing the European Communities: Treaties Amending These Treaties; Documents Concerning the Accession (Luxembourg, 1973).

Commission

"Annual Economic Review 1980–81," *European Economy*, No. 7 (November 1980), pp. 29–129.
"Annual Economic Review 1982–83," *European Economy*, No. 14 (November 1982), pp. 33–148.
"The European Monetary System-Commentary, Documents," *European Economy*, No. 3 (July 1979), pp. 63–111.
"European Monetary System: The First Six Months," *European Economy*, No. 4 (November 1979), pp. 79–81.
"The European Monetary System and Monetary Policy in the European Community," *European Economy*, No. 10 (November 1981), pp. 72–92.
"Documents Relating to the European Monetary System," *European Economy*, No. 12 (July 1982).
Jenkins, Roy, "Europe's Present Challenge and Future Opportunity," speech delivered in Florence, October 27, 1977.
———, "The European Monetary System: Recent Experience and Future Prospects," speech delivered in Rome, October 1980.

Monetary Committee

Monetary Committee, *Compendium of Community Monetary Texts, 1979* (Luxembourg, 1979).

Official Journal

Official Journal of the European Communities: Information and Notices, C 124, Vol. 24 (May 25, 1981).

National Authorities

Bank of England, "Intervention Arrangements in the European Monetary System," *Quarterly Review*, Vol. 19 (June 1979), pp. 190–94.
Banque de France, "Le Système Monétaire Européen," Service de l'Information (May 1979), pp. 1–15.
Banque Nationale de Belgique, "Le Système Monétaire Européen," *Bulletin* (July-August, 1979).
Central Bank of Ireland, "A Guide to the Arithmetic of the EMS Exchange-Rate Mechanism," *Quarterly Bulletin* (Autumn 1979), pp. 76–100.
Deutsche Bundesbank, "The European Monetary System: Structure and Operation," *Monthly Report of the Deutsche Bundesbank*, Vol. 31 (March 1979), pp. 11–18.
France, Ministère de l'Economie, "Le Système Monétaire Européen," Service de l'Information (April 1979).
United Kingdom, Chancellor of the Exchequer, *The European Monetary System*, Presented to Parliament by the Chancellor of the Exchequer by command of Her Majesty, November 1978 (London, H.M. Stationery Office, 1978), Command Paper No. 7405.

Selected Other Publications

Abraham, Jean-Paul and Michel Vanden Abeele, eds., *Système monétaire européen et réforme monétaire mondiale: European Monetary System and International Monetary Reform* (Editions de l'Université de Bruxelles, 1981).
Banca Nazionale del Lavoro, "The European Monetary System: The First Two Years," *Quarterly Review*, Vol. 34 (September 1981), pp. 261–370. Proceedings of the Fourth International Seminar on European Economic and Monetary Union, held at Danmarks Nationalbank, Copenhagen, March 13-14, 1981.

APPENDIX II • BIBLIOGRAPHY

Baquiast, Henri, "The European Monetary System and International Monetary Relations" (with comments by Robert Solomon) in *The European Monetary System: Its Promise and Prospects*, Papers Prepared for a Conference held at the Brookings Institution in April 1979, ed. by Philip H. Trezise (The Brookings Institution, Washington, 1979), pp. 49–59.

Cohen, Benjamin J., *The European Monetary System: An Outsider's View*, Essays in International Finance, No. 142, International Finance Section, Princeton University (1981).

de Vries, Tom, *On the Meaning and Future of the European Monetary System*, Essays in International Finance, No. 138, International Finance Section, Princeton University (1980).

Dennis, Geoffrey E.J., "United Kingdom's Monetary Independence and Membership of the European Monetary System," in *Système monétaire europèen et réforme monètaire mondiale: European Monetary System and International Monetary Reform*, ed. by Jean-Paul Abraham and Michel Vanden Abeele (Editions de l'Université de Bruxelles, 1981), pp. 139–56.

Emerson, Michael, "European Dimensions in the Problems of Adjustment," *Système monétaire européen et réforme monétaire mondiale: European Monetary System and International Monetary Reform* (Editions de l' Université de Bruxelles, 1981), pp. 107–38.

Gold, Joseph, *SDRs, Currencies, and Gold—Fourth Survey of New Legal Developments*, Pamphlet Series, No. 33, International Monetary Fund (Washington, 1980), pp. 46–64.

Haberer, Jean-Yves, "Les problèmes de l'identité monétaire Européenne," *La Revue des Deux Mondes* (March 1981).

Kloten, Norbert, "Zur 'Endphase' des Europäischen Währungssystems," *Internationale Anpassungsprozesse*, Schriften des Vereins für Socialpolitik, Neue Folge Band 114 (1981).

Ludlow, Peter, *The Making of the European Monetary System: A Case Study of the Politics of the European Community*, Butterworth Scientific (London, 1982).

McCarthy, Colin, "EMS and the End of Ireland's Sterling Link," *Lloyds Bank Review* No. 136 (April 1980), pp. 30–42.

McMahon, Christopher, "The Long-Run Implications of the European Monetary System" (with comments by William J. Fellner) in *The European Monetary System: Its Promise and Prospects*, Papers Prepared for a Conference held at the Brookings Institution in April 1979, ed. by Philip H. Trezise (The Brookings Institution, Washington, 1979), pp. 81–96.

Marsh, David, "Sterling and the European Monetary System," *The Banker*, Vol. 129 (September 1979), pp. 41–43.

Masera, Rainer S., "The Operation of the EMS: A European View," *Economia Internationale* (November 1979).

———, "The First Two Years of the EMS: The Exchange-Rate Experience," in "The European Monetary System: The First Two Years," Banca Nazionale del Lavoro, *Quarterly Review*, Vol. 34 (September 1981), pp. 271–86.

Murray, C.H., "The European Monetary System–Implications for Ireland," Central Bank of Ireland, *Annual Report*, 1979.

Ortoli, François-Xavier, "The European Community Looks at Monetary Integration," Deutsche Bundesbank, *Auszüge aus Presseartikeln*, No. 15 (February 26, 1979), pp. 3–5.

Padoa-Schioppa, Tommaso, "The EMF: Topics for Discussion," Proceedings of the Second International Seminar on European Economic and Monetary Union, Geneva, December 7–8, 1979, Banca Nazionale del Lavoro, *Quarterly Review*, Vol. 33 (September 1980), pp. 317–43.

Polak, J.J., "The EMF: External Relations," Proceedings of the Second International Seminar on European Economic and Monetary Union, Geneva, December 7–8, 1979, Banca Nazionale del Lavoro, *Quarterly Review*, Vol. 33 (September 1980), pp. 359–72.

Rey, Jean-Jacques, "Les Techniques du Système Monétaire Européen," *Aussenwirtschaft*, Vol. 34 (June 1979), pp. 158–64.

———, "Some Comments on the Merits and Limits of the Indicator of Divergence of the European Monetary System," *Revue de la Banque*, No. 1 (1982), pp. 3–15.

Rieke, Wolfgang, "Das Europäische Währungssystem," Deutsche Bundesbank, *Auszüge aus Presseartikeln* (March 17, 1980).

Salop, Joanne, "The Divergence Indicator: A Technical Note," International Monetary Fund, *Staff Papers*, Vol. 28 (December 1981), pp. 682–97.

Schlüter, Peter-W., "Die ECU und der Europäische Währungsfonds," *Integration* 2/82 (April 1982), pp. 54–73.

Scholl, Franz, "Praktische Erfahrungen mit dem Europäischen Währungssystem," *Probleme der Währungspolitik*, Schriften des Vereins für Socialpolitik, Neue Folge Band 120, 1981, pp. 151–71.

Solomon, Robert, "An American View of the EMS," Deutsche Bundesbank, *Auszüge aus Presseartikeln*, No. 15 (February 26, 1979), pp. 6–7.

Thygesen, Niels, "The Emerging European Monetary System: Precursors, First Steps and Policy Options," in "EMS: The Emerging European Monetary System," Papers and Proceedings of the First International Seminar on the EMS held at Louvain-la-Neuve, March 24–25, 1979, by John Williamson, Alexandre Lamfalussy, Niels Thygesen, et.al. Ed. by Robert Triffin. *Bulletin de la Banque Nationale de Belgique* (April 1979), pp. 87–125.

———, "Are Monetary Policies and Performances Converging?" (with a comment by Wolfgang Rieke) in "The European Monetary System: The First Two Years," Banca Nazionale del Lavoro, *Quarterly Review*, Vol. 34 (September 1981), pp. 297–326.

Trezise, Philip H., ed., *The European Monetary System: Its Promise and Prospects*, Papers Prepared for a Conference held at the Brookings Institution in April 1979 (The Brookings Institution, Washington, 1979).

Triffin, Robert, "The European Monetary System and How it Fits into the International Monetary System," *Economia*, Vol. 3 (Lisbon, October 1979), pp. 537–61.

Ungerer, Horst, "The European Monetary System," International Monetary Fund, *IMF Survey, Supplement* (March 19, 1979), pp. 97–100.

U.S. Congress, Joint Economic Committee and Committee on Banking, Finance, and Urban Affairs, *The European Monetary System: Problems and Prospects*, 96th Congress, 1st Session (Washington, Government Printing Office, 1979).

van Ypersele de Strihou, Jacques, "The Future of the European Monetary System," *Revue de la Banque*, No. 2 (1981), pp. 179–95.

Vaubel, Roland, "The Return to the New European Monetary System: Objectives, Incentives, Perspectives," *Monetary Institutions and the Policy Process*, Carnegie-Rochester Conference Series on Public Policy, Vol. 13 (Autumn, 1980), pp. 173–221.

Werner, Pierre, "Du Plan Werner au système monétaire européen," *Bulletin de documentation*, Service Information et Presse, Luxembourg (March 1980), pp. 1–7.

Williamson, John, Alexandre Lamfalussy, Niels Thygesen, et. al., "EMS: The Emerging European Monetary System," Papers and Proceedings of the First International Seminar on the EMS held at Louvain-la-Neuve, March 24–25, 1979. Ed. by Robert Triffin. *Bulletin de la Banque Nationale de Belgique* (April 1979), pp. 3–186.

Occasional Papers of the International Monetary Fund

1. International Capital Markets: Recent Developments and Short-Term Prospects, by a Staff Team Headed by R.C. Williams, Exchange and Trade Relations Department. 1980.

2. Economic Stabilization and Growth in Portugal, by Hans O. Schmitt. 1981.

3. External Indebtedness of Developing Countries, by a Staff Team Headed by Bahram Nowzad and Richard C. Williams. 1981.

4. World Economic Outlook: A Survey by the Staff of the International Monetary Fund. 1981.

5. Trade Policy Developments in Industrial Countries, by S.J. Anjaria, Z. Iqbal, L.L. Perez, and W.S. Tseng. 1981.

6. The Multilateral System of Payments: Keynes, Convertibility, and the International Monetary Fund's Articles of Agreement, by Joseph Gold. 1981.

7. International Capital Markets: Recent Developments and Short-Term Prospects, 1981, by a Staff Team Headed by Richard C. Williams, with G.G. Johnson. 1981.

8. Taxation in Sub-Saharan Africa. Part I: Tax Policy and Administration in Sub-Saharan Africa, by Carlos A. Aguirre, Peter S. Griffith, and M. Zühtü Yücelik. Part II: A Statistical Evaluation of Taxation in Sub-Saharan Africa, by Vito Tanzi. 1981.

9. World Economic Outlook: A Survey by the Staff of the International Monetary Fund. 1982.

10. International Comparisons of Government Expenditure, by Alan A. Tait and Peter S. Heller. 1982.

11. Payments Arrangements and the Expansion of Trade in Eastern and Southern Africa, by Shailendra J. Anjaria, Sena Eken, and John F. Laker. 1982.

12. Effects of Slowdown in Industrial Countries on Growth in Non-Oil Developing Countries, by Morris Goldstein and Mohsin S. Khan. 1982.

13. Currency Convertibility in the Economic Community of West African States, by John B. McLenaghan, Saleh M. Nsouli, and Klaus-Walter Riechel. 1982.

14. International Capital Markets: Developments and Prospects, 1982, by a Staff Team Headed by Richard C. Williams, with G.G. Johnson. 1982.

15. Hungary: An Economic Survey, by a Staff Team Headed by Patrick de Fontenay. 1982.

16. Developments in International Trade Policy, by S.J. Anjaria, Z. Iqbal, N. Kirmani, and L.L. Perez. 1982.

17. Aspects of the International Banking Safety Net, by G.G. Johnson, with Richard K. Abrams. 1983.

18. Oil Exporters' Economic Development in an Interdependent World, by Jahangir Amuzegar. 1983.

19. The European Monetary System: The Experience, 1979–82, by Horst Ungerer, with Owen Evans and Peter Nyberg.

International Monetary Fund, Washington, D.C. 20431, U.S.A.
Telephone number: 202 477 2945
Cable address: Interfund